JOHN AND DAV

ELERS

and their Contemporaries

by

GORDON ELLIOTT

JOHN PHILIP ELERS

Engraving of Wedgwood's portrait medallion of John Philip Elers, commissioned by his son Paul Elers. This led to Wedgwood's letter to Bentley (1771) in which he identifies the brothers' contribution to potting in North Staffordshire. (see page 17).

JP

Produced by
Jonathan Horne Publications
66c Kensington Church Street
London W8 4BY

Telephone : 0171 221 5658
Facsimile : 0171 792 3090

CONTENTS

ACKNOWLEDGEMENTS

Special thanks are due to the Potteries Museum, Stoke-on-Trent for supplying several key illustrations in this work, with a thank you to Miranda Goodby and David Barker for assisting access to this material.

I am also indebted to Christopher Green for information concerning the excavations carried out at Dwight's Fulham Pottery. Jonathan Horne exceeded his responsibilities as a publisher by obtaining many of the photographs which he has researched and provided the captions. For this I am extremely grateful.

Others who have supplied photographs and related information include Luke Beckerdite, Tamsin Daniel, Leslie Grigsby, Michael Gillingham, Denis Haselgrove, Robin Hildyard, Amanda Lange, Margaret Macfarlane, Errol Manners, Jacqui Pearce, Richard Coleman-Smith and Peter Williams. I also thank Nicholas Wells and Simon Westman for their patience in typing parts of the manuscript.

Finally, I must thank Sheila, my wife, for her support during decades of self-indulgence researching this and numerous other ceramic history projects.

Gordon Elliott, 1998.

INTRODUCTION

Simeon Shaw, writing in the 1820s, identified the transitional role of the Elers brothers' activities in Staffordshire.[1] That the work does not include any illustrations is unfortunate because it will be argued that product identification is fundamental to any assessment of their achievements. Later authorities from Llewellyn Jewitt to R.L. Hobson went further than Shaw in attributing a somewhat disparate group of red stonewares to the Elers' Bradwell Wood pottery, many of which are undoubtedly of a later date.[2]

The first serious attempt at an accurate classification was undertaken by W.B. Honey with the publication of a paper in the *Transactions of the English Ceramic Circle* in 1934.[3] In adopting an approach based upon stylistic features he was able to separate the later eighteenth century Staffordshire red stoneware products, by such potters as Astbury and Whieldon, from wares that reveal obvious origins in the seventeenth century blanc de chine porcelains of China, and European silver and pewter forms of this date. Despite the importance of William Honey's paper it still left unanswered questions created by the need to differentiate between what might have been made by the Elers and John Dwight. It was with these points in mind that I began my research in connection with the Elers' short period in Staffordshire.

In May, 1955 I carried out a small scale archaeological investigation in the area surrounding Bradwell Hall, the purpose of which was to reveal any evidence of early structures no longer apparent on the surface, plus wasters resulting from the Elers' production. This approach was, in part, motivated by Simeon Shaw's statement that 'The foundations (of an oven) were very distinctly to be seen in 1808, tho' now covered by an enlargement of the barn.[4] He goes on to report that 'E. Wood and J. Riley, Esqrs. both separately measured the inside diameter of the remains which were at about five feet; while the ovens, of the same date, in Burslem, were ten or twelve feet. My excavation was somewhat handicapped by changes that had

taken place on the site since 1808. For example, the barn referred to had been replaced by a prefabricated structure which was not necessarily located on the same site as that visited by Enoch Wood and John Riley. As might have been expected this particular aspect of my investigation proved fruitless. Additional trial holes were sunk which, fortunately, revealed seventy small fragments of red stoneware and a base fragment from a German grey salt-glazed mug.[6] Although the then owner (Mr Twigge) was never less than generous in allowing me access to most parts of the site further investigation was limited by circumstances created by a working farm.

An active interest in the Elers was not renewed until some twenty years later when my curatorial duties involved a re-appraisal of the Stoke-on-Trent City Museum's collection of red stonewares. As attribution came into the exercise it was necessary to categorize the wares with reference to criteria identified by W.B. Honey. In addition to stylistic considerations I also classified the pots on the basis of whether they had been formed by throwing or press moulding. It was apparent that the majority had been thrown, while some two or three forms were clearly the products of a procedure involving plastic clay in conjunction with a mould; probably of plaster-of-Paris. The engine-turned wares in the museum collection, relatable to Wedgwood, were obviously later than the rest and although lacking the usual Wedgwood mark, impressed with metal type, were, nevertheless, clearly from his Burslem (pre 1769) period.[7]

Having carefully examined every red stoneware item in the museum I was, on the basis of Honey's approach, able to identify two pieces as belonging to the late seventeenth century. This stage of the exercise was also concerned with establishing criteria that would lead to an objective assessment of their transitional role in the Staffordshire context, an objective that involved a parallel appraisal of the local products being produced in Staffordshire prior to the Elers' arrival at Bradwell Hall.

Engraved by J.T.Wedgwood

Dimsdale Hall (reputedly the Elers' residence during their period in Staffordshire), as it appeared in the early nineteenth century. From John Ward's History of the Borough of Stoke-upon-Trent, 1843.

It seemed appropriate at the time to start by reading the works of other historians who had offered information on what was clearly an obligatory subject for anyone attempting a history of ceramic manufacture in Staffordshire.[8] Perhaps, inevitably, I began with Simeon Shaw, a source that has been used by many writers from Jewitt to Bernard Rackham. Few, however, have been prepared to accept his information without reservation. Rackham's estimation of Shaw is not unrepresentative *'our confidence in this writer's assertions is shaken not only by the slovenly and ill-coordinated manner in which the facts and events are set down but also by the statements which can be shown to be palpably untrue'.*[9] Unfortunately, Shaw was overdependent on *'the Reminiscences of many aged Persons, who had witnessed the time and manner in which the Art of Pottery had attained much of its importance'.*[10] It should be said that he was writing at a period

before the establishment of public libraries in North Staffordshire, and prior to the existence of a county records office to which the public had access.[11] Although clearly not relevant to the Elers, Shaw was also largely motivated by a desire to please those in a position to purchase (in most cases contemporary pottery manufacturers) one or several copies of his book, a situation that was not, perhaps, conducive to objectivity and historical accuracy.

Even Shaw felt it necessary to mention that in assessing the Elers' importance others who, incidentally, he chose not to identify, had resorted to *'much hyperbole'* in their treatment of the subject. There is an obvious emphasis on the secrecy that allegedly surrounded their work at Bradwell Wood. He tells the reader that; *'A very singular method of ascertaining all their processes, is currently reported to have been adopted by another person named Astbury ..... Having*

4

assumed the garb and appearance of an idiot, with all proper vacancy of countenance, he presented himself before the manufacturers at Bradwell, and submitted to the cuffs, kicks, and unkind treatment of masters and workmen, with a ludicrous grimace, as the proof of the extent of his mental ability.[12] To reinforce the secrecy theme Shaw proceeds by mentioning the brothers' use of a novel 'mode of communication' between their residence at Dimsdale Hall and scene of operations at Bradwell Wood, a distance of approximately one mile. Later writers went a stage further in identifying the *'mode'* as a speaking tube, and in the case of G.W. and F.A. Rhead illustrate what they claimed to be actual sections from it in their book, *Staffordshire Pots and Potters*. In Stoke-on-Trent City Museum there is a single section of tube which, according to an inscription in pencil, was appropriately *'discovered at Bradwell Wood.'* It is unfortunate for the Rhead's credibility that the item was clearly formed by extrusion, and is in a composition that, in keeping with the production method, is much later than the 1690s.[13]

The employment of *'simpletons'* and use of a speaking tube is information introduced to reinforce the secrecy idea, a notion that is compatible with the claim that the brothers' used technically complex procedures. Shaw states that Astbury *'On returning home each evening ..... formed models of the several kinds of implements, and made memorandums of the processes; which practice he continued a considerable time (near two years is mentioned) until he ascertained that no further information was likely to be obtained'.*[14]

Jewitt, writing some thirty plus years after Shaw, endorses much of his account to an extent that large extracts are reproduced from the 1829 work without amendments.[15] Indeed, other later writers have drawn from Shaw without questioning his historical accuracy, except in instances where his information conflicted with their own.[16]

The Rhead's assessment of the Elers is in some respects more controversial than Shaw's. For example, as designers involved in the day-to day running of a major factory, their statement that *'The salt-glazing process does not give off dense smoke'* is obviously incorrect.[17] Certain subsequent pronouncements on technical matters are also, arguably, misinformed. It is interesting to compare their information on the Elers with that of J.C. Wedgwood. Despite working under similar limitations, with regard to documentary evidence, Wedgwood, nevertheless, succeeded in providing an account of the Elers that to the modern reader is more measured and objective.[18]

While these writers often differed in their respective interpretation of issues they shared a common limitation in their confusion regarding the attribution of seventeenth and eighteenth century red stonewares. That this was a long-standing problem is mentioned by R.L. Hobson in the British Museum's *A Guide to the English Pottery and Porcelain*, 1904, to quote his comments; *'No marks were used by the Elers, except, perhaps, those imitation Chinese seal marks which are found on red ware of all periods;* (appendix 5) *consequently, the identification of their work is very difficult.'*

I propose to show that with reference to documentary sources, object analysis, and the re-creation of a production process, involving clay from the same deposits as those used by the Elers, it has, indeed, proved possible to offer answers to matters raised by contributors to ceramic history from Simeon Shaw to William Honey.

Originally thought to have been a section from the 'Elers speaking tube'. The composition and evidence of production by extrusion indicate a post 1850 date. Courtesy Potteries Museum.

NOTES TO INTRODUCTION

1. Simeon Shaw, *History of the Staffordshire Potteries*, Hanley, 1829. Hereafter referred to as Shaw, Staffordshire Potteries.

2. L. Jewitt, *The Ceramic Art of Great Britain*, 1877, Poole, New Orchard Editions reprint, 1985, p.75, figs. 318-319.

R.L. Hobson, *Catalogue of the Collection of English Pottery*, British Museum, 1903, Plate XVIII. Hereafter referred to as Hobson, British Museum.

3. W.B. Honey, "Elers' Ware", *English Ceramic Circle Transactions*, No. II, 1934. Hereafter referred to as Honey, Elers' Ware.

4. Reported in the *Transactions of the North Staffordshire Field Club*, Vol. XCI, 1956-57, p.96.

5. Shaw, *Staffordshire Potteries*, p.121.

6. In the reserve collections, Stoke-on-Trent City Museum.

7. Engine turning in connection with British ceramics was introduced by Wedgwood during the 1760s. The idea was based upon a principle initially applied to areas of metalworking. For further information on Wedgwood's early experiments regarding the production of a lathe for this purpose see Ann Finer and George Savage, *The Selected Letters of Josiah Wedgwood*, London, Cory, Adams and Mackay, 1965, p.27. Hereafter referred to as Finer and Savage, Wedgwood Letters.

8. G.W. and F.A. Rhead, *Staffordshire Pots and Potters*, London, Hutchinson, 1906. Hereafter to be referred to as Rhead, Staffordshire Pots & Potters.

L.M. Solon, *The Art of the Old English Potter*, London, Bemrose, 1885. Hereafter referred to as Solon, Art of Old English Potter.

9. Bernard Rackham, *Early Staffordshire Pottery*, London, Faber, 1951, p.3. Hereafter referred to as Rackham, Staffordshire Pottery.

10. Shaw, *Staffordshire Potteries*, p.5, 11.

11. The William Salt Library was founded in 1872.

12. Shaw, *Staffordshire Potteries*, p.119.

13. Extruded pipes and electrical porcelains post-date 1850.

14. Shaw, *Staffordshire Potteries*, p.120.

15. L. Jewitt, *The Wedgwoods: Being a Life of Josiah Wedgwood*, London, Virtue, 1865.

16. Even Bernard Rackham, despite his unambiguous disdain for Shaw as an historical source, endorses information in his *Early Staffordshire Pottery* that is clearly traceable to him.

17. The introduction of salt to a potter's oven is followed by the emission of a sodium chloride vapour. Salting, with its attendant pollution of the atmosphere, has been commented upon by Shaw, *Staffordshire Potteries*, and J.F. Blacker, *The A.B.C. of English Salt-Glaze Stoneware from Dwight to Doulton*, London, 1922.

18. J.C. Wedgwood, *Staffordshire Pottery and Its History*, London, Sampson Low, Marston, 1913.

CHAPTER 1 : THE PRINCIPAL PLAYERS

John Philip Elers and his older brother David were Dutch born silversmiths who came to London in the 1680's where since 1675 their father Martin had had a shop selling *Esprit de Porcellane* (probably a type of white glass). Their uncle also had a shop in the city of London selling *lackery* ware (appendix 6). In 1686 a David Elers opened shop at the sign of the Crown and Sceptre near St. Clement's London selling silver. Sometime prior to 1693 the brothers had set up a pottery at Vauxhall *(Foxhall)* and were producing slipcast saltglaze stoneware from local clays (plate 1). They also had access to the Staffordshire red clay and it seems likely they had moved into Dimsdale Hall Staffordshire by about 1690-91 with their works about 1 mile away at Bradwell Wood. It is assumed that John was probably the potter whilst David ran the business.

By 1698 the brothers had relinquished their lease at Bradwell Wood and moved to Vauxhall where they were declared bankrupt in 1700 and their property sold to pay the debts. John went on to Dublin and was set up in business by a Lady Barrington. Between 1715 and 1722 it seems that he was being supplied with quantities of oriental porcelain acquired by his brother David from the East India Company in London. Although their potting in England was of short duration they did achieve a quality in their unglazed red stoneware that would not be equalled for some seventy years.

The theatrical metaphor adopted in naming this chapter is a reflection of the way the Elers, in particular, were described by some writers during the early nineteenth century. In the case of Simeon Shaw it produced such stories as the brothers' use of an unspecified form of communication between their residence and potworks at Bradwell Wood, plus the alleged feigned *'idiocy'* of Astbury and Twyford. Some seventy-four years later George Elers included a short section in his autobiography where he provided an account of John Philip and David Elers and their antecedents' intimate links with some of the leading Royal families of Europe. An element of drama is even suggested by the circumstances preceding and resulting from Dwight's lawsuit taken out against the Elers in 1693.

John Dwight who had set up his pottery at Fulham in 1672 claimed to have discovered *'the mystery of stoneware'* and received a sole right of production in this country. Dwight's patents were vigorously defended and lawsuits were taken out against at least 11 different potters. The lawsuit dated 20 June 1693 cited John Chandler, John Philip Elers, David Elers and James Morley. Dwight's main contention in this case was that John Chandler, whom he had employed as a labourer, had been enticed away by others and had revealed his secrets.[1] The result of the case was that the Elers were compelled to produce their red stoneware under licence. James Morley of Nottingham played a relatively minor role in this drama and seems to have been little affected by the lawsuit. He is less often discussed by writers on ceramic history which suggests a more distant connection with Dwight than that of his contemporaries. Morley is remembered for his fine quality salt-glazed stoneware, an advertisement of c. 1700 shows his 'carved' wares (Plate 13A, B) as well as a turned 'decanter' and 'mogg'. (Bodlian Library, Oxford). The Dwight/Elers connection therefore consists on the one part of an impressive innovator with an ambition to raise the status of ceramic production in Britain, in terms of both the maker and product, compared with the recent arrivals from abroad who as we will see claimed aristocratic connections and an interest in chemistry. If Dwight's claims were justified, and there appears to have been little doubt they were, the Elers benefited from the defection of his ex-employee, John Chandler.

The Bradwell Elers biographical details form a small part of a manuscript said to have been discovered by George Levenson Gower in the library at Burton Hall, Staffordshire, having originally been compiled as an autobiography by Captain George Elers of the 12th. Regiment of Foot who, we are told, 'expired' at St. Helier on Jersey in January 1842 'from a stroke of apoplexy.' It appears that during the period immediately prior to his death the author was living in greatly reduced circumstances *'as practically his sole means of subsistence was a trifling annuity from a cousin, Mrs. Tennant. In fact beyond a few watches and a little jewellry he had only a small sum of ready cash.'* The last years of George Elers' life were in marked contrast to the social standing claimed for his seventeenth century ancestors. In the absence of corroborative evidence it is impossible to say whether these claims were justified or made merely in an attempt to elevate the family to an aristocratic status.

As the information on his potting ancestors forms a relatively minor part (pp.1-4) of the complete text it is presented here as in the original version.

'The old baronial family of Elers were long settled in the northern parts of Lower Saxony, where many places preserve lasting memorials of the fact by the names they bear, as Elersdorf, Elerswolf, Elers-dorpt, and others of similar terminology. In Hamburg some hereditary post of honour and distinction were (sic) long held by the family; one of them was Admiral of the Fleet, which during the existence of the Hanseatic League in its full vigour was the most considerable maritime force in Europe. He married a daughter of the Prince of Baden, in Germany, some of the honours of which family the son of that marriage asserted his right to in a long and expensive lawsuit, which in the Aulic Council of the Empire was determined against him. Disgusted with the decision, the family suddenly removed into Holland, where my great-great-grandfather, Martin Elers, was born, in the year 1621, and in 1650 married the daughter of Daniel van Mildert, a merchant of eminence, who brought with her a large fortune. Van Mildert was a person of such mercantile importance that the Queen of Charles I, Henrietta Maria, during her residence in Holland in the time of her misfortunes, occasionally resided with him, and his little daughter, afterwards the wife of Martin Elers, recollects sitting in Her Majesty's lap eating sweetmeats at her father's table. This Martin Elers afterwards went as Ambassador from Holland to the Emperor of Germany. The eldest son of this marriage was my great-grandfather, John Philip, a godson of the Elector of Maintz, of the illustrious family of Schonbrunn, who is honourably mentioned in Lord Clarendon's History. This John Philip associated much with men of science; was a great chemist, and the intimate friend and associate of Joachim Becker, the most distinguished person in Chemical researches of his time, and of whom Boerhave, in his Chemical Lectures, speaks with the greatest respect and regard. Their pictures were mutually exchanged, and some of his books were dedicated to my great grandfather. The celebrated Christina, Queen of Sweden, was his godmother, and held him in her arms at the baptismal font, and we had a family picture recording the fact. She treated him with the greatest kind-ness and affection, and constantly called him her cousin, in rememberance of his descent from the royal House of Baden. The Elector of Maintz presented him with a service of plate and his picture set round with large rubies and diamonds, which my grandfather possessed. This John Philip Elers was born at Utrecht, September 7, 1664. He had an elder brother named David, born in Amsterdam, June 13, 1656. He also was a man devoted to the sciences, and particularly to chemistry. He travelled all over Europe, and visited Moscow among other places. His brother, Philip, also travelled a great deal, associating with men of science. Both of them being great chemists, they in Holland were taught, or found out, the secret of mixing clay, and on their settling in England they introduced it into Staffordshire, and imparted their discovery to Mr. Wedgwood, who there established his famous potteries, which are still in existence. On their arrival in England, about the time of the Revolution, they settled in Staffordshire, and took up their residence at a large house called Brada Hall, which they rented off Mr. Sneyd, of Keele, where my great-grandfather married Miss Elizabeth Banks, whose sister at that time was married to the Rev. Edward Vernon [2] and ancestor of the noble Baron of that title. The Prince of Orange, afterwards William III, honoured him with his esteem and friendship, and granted to a brother of his wife a pension of £300 per anum. His sister Sarah was the second wife of Sir William Phipps, Governor of New England, who founded the present noble family of Mulgrave.

My great-grandfather was married in Leicestershire August 26, 1699, and soon afterwards went to reside in Battersea, in Surrey. In 1701 my great-grandfather removed from

Surrey to Dublin, where he remained until his death in 1738. The other brother, David resided in London, and was buried at Battersea, 1742. Whether my grandfather was born in England or Ireland I know not, but he finished his education at the University of Oxford, and was considered a very accomplished scholar.[3] He made law his profession, and was called to the Bar soon after he left Oxford.'

In view of the possible inaccuracies contained in George Elers' account of his ancestors it is difficult not to treat the above grandiose claims with a considerable degree of scepticism. Evidence from contemporary documentary sources, such as advertisements and lawsuits, is more reliable in providing a chronological framework for the Elers in Britain.

Several writers have suggested that the brothers' presence in London coincided with William lll's acceptance of Whig and Tory invitations to invade England in 1688. However, an advertisement in the *London Gazette* indicates that at least David Elers was present in the capital some two years earlier; *'About a Month since, was stopt by Mr. David Elers at the Crown and Scepter near St. Clements Church, a Silver Cup, and not any Body enquiring after it since, these are to give Notice, that the right Owner may have it again, paying the Charges, and describing the Marks'.[4]*

That David Elers was not the first member of his family to live in England is made apparent in a letter written by J.B. Crafft in 1672 to Gottfried Willhelm Leibniz (1648-1716) the eminent German philosopher and mathematician, in which he mentions the brothers' father, Martin Elers owning a shop where *'East Indian rarities are sold'*. Some three years later, in 1675, the same correspondent, writing from Hanover, reports that *'white glass'* which he named *'Esprit de Porcellane'* was also being sold by Martin Elers in London[5] According to an advertisement in the *London Gazette* for the 2-6 December, 1686 a David Elers owned another shop at the sign of the Crown and Sceptre, near St. Clement's Church in London, where he dealt in silver. Theodore or Dirck Elers (died 1693) an uncle of the brothers, was a merchant in china and *'lackery'* at St Mary le Bow in the City of London (appendix 6). Although there is no known family relationship others named Elers were residing in England prior to 1688. The nineteenth century

designer and ceramic historian, L.M. Solon identified the existence of parliamentary records for the House of Commons 'in which is recorded for January 1680, an engrossed bill for the naturalisation of *"Peter Elers and others aliens born".*[6]

A later document, in this instance a pass, was issued in 1690 to enable *'Mr. David Ellers'* and Philip Gibbon to travel to Holland on the 9 August.[7] In the following year we have evidence of the first Elers' link with North Staffordshire when it was reported in the Corporation Minutes for Newcastle-under-Lyme, 18 August, 1691, that it was *'Ordered that a present be made to my Lord Chiefe Justice Holt at his cominge to this Burrough from Lancaster Assizes of some of Mr. David Elers earthen ware to the vallew of three pounds or thereabouts'.[8]* Although not mentioned by Simeon Shaw, and other nineteenth century writers, this event was perfectly compatible with their belief that the Elers were actively obtaining clay in north Staffordshire from 1690. Conversely, terms contained in Dwight's 1693 lawsuit have given rise to the more recent opinion that they were not working at Bradwell before 1693.[9]

Evidence in the lawsuits, and contemporary accounts suggest that the Elers maintained a London connection throughout the period of their involvement with ceramic production in Staffordshire, and although described as living in Fulham their pottery was situated in Vauxhall. A Vauxhall location is reinforced by John Houghton's 'Advertisement' in *Husbandry and Trade Improv'd* for the 13 October, 1693. He records; *'There is found near Faux-hall in Surrey, a sort of Clay used to make all sorts of Tea Pots ..... by two Dutch brothers whose names are Eelers.'* (Plate I). Upon initial consideration this information would appear to be undermined by a communication to the Royal Society by Martin Lister dated May 1 1693, in which he mentions the Elers and the nature of their products; *'These are made of English Haemitites in Staffordshire, as I take it, by two Dutch-men incomparable Artists'.* If, however, David remained in London while John Philip moved to Staffordshire, we have a feasible explanation for Houghton's and Lister's (appendix 3) seemingly contradictory information. This possible aspect of the brothers' working relationship has been accepted since the nineteenth century; *'..... and it is probable that while David was selling the ware at his shop in the "Poultry", John Philip was manufacturing it at Bradwell Wood'*.[10] While L.M. Solon does not offer any evidence to support his theory Rhoda Edwards believes that an answer lies in the wording of the agreement drawn up at the termination of the Elers' lease of Bradwell Hall which states that the premises were *'now or late .... in the possession of John Elers gent'*.[11] Taking all the documentary evidence into account we are left with a situation that suggests the Elers' use of the Bradwell clay from circa 1690, hence their claim in reply to Dwight's first lawsuit (20 June, 1693) to have been in the business of making red stoneware and, indeed, saltglaze products *'for about the space of three years now last past'*. This scenario would accommodate the previously mentioned presentation to Lord Chief Justice Holt in 1691. The decision that led to John Philip moving to Staffordshire in November, 1693 was an aspect of the resolution of their dispute with John Dwight.[12]

The next significant date in the Elers chronology is recorded in the journal of diarist and traveller Celia Fiennes who, upon enquiring about their potworks and products in 1698, was informed that they, or as is more likely, John Philip, had left the area. She *'went to Newcastle in Staffordshire to see the makeing the fine tea potts cups and saucers of the fine red earth, in imitation and as curious as that which comes from China, but was defeated in my design, they comeing to an end of their clay they made use off for that sort of ware and therefore was remov'd to some other place where they were not settled at their work, so could not see it; therefore I went on ....'*

The last known Elers' link with Staffordshire occurred in 1697 when on the 26 August John Philip married Elizabeth Banks of Uttoxeter. Some three years later (1700) the brothers' failure to establish a profitable pottery-making business was made apparent by the appearance of a notice in the *London Gazette*,[13] *'A Commission of Bankrupt being awarded against David Elers, and John-Philip Elers, late of Foxhall in Surrey ...'*.According to George Elers they were given financial help in 1701 by a Lady Barrington who assisted John in the setting up of a merchant's business in Dublin.[14] This apparent uplift in their fortunes was shortlived for personal tragedy

followed with the death of Elizabeth Elers in 1702.[15] The later years of David and John Philip's lives are less well documented than the period of their work in Staffordshire. It is largely to their dispute with John Dwight that we are indebted for the body of documented events that preceded the events culminating in their bankruptcy.

While Simeon Shaw's account of the Elers makes no reference to their links with Dwight later writers have generally made due acknowledgement to the lawsuits and the Elers' alleged association with his ex employee, John Chandler. That the work being undertaken at Fulham would have attracted the Dutchmens' attention was almost inevitable given Dwight's status as a potter and scientist in late seventeenth century London; scientific credentials that are further reinforced with reference to his working relationship with the eminent Oxford academic, Robert Boyle. It is, I believe, conceivable that the Elers had been in contact with Dwight prior to the events immediately preceding the lawsuits. For example, their scientific activites (a claim made by George Elers) might have indirectly introduced them to members of the Royal Society. Is it possible that this circle included non-members similarly involved, one of whom was John Dwight ? What might have been discussed in the context of laboratory experiments with novel materials, in this case the red clay or haemitites from Bradwell Wood, was of direct interest to the brothers in their ambition to imitate the Yixing wares of China. If Dwight had described his experiments either publicly or in private, in the presence of the brothers, it would have alerted them to the existence of haemititic clays in North Staffordshire. Conflict between the parties inevitably arose later as a result of these interests taking on a commercial dimension.

John Dwight's wider reputation was largely determined by his successful registration of patents for salt-glazed stoneware. Previous writers on this subject have offered evidence to suggest that while he was probably the first potter in Britain to have manufactured such wares on a commercial scale (from circa 1675) others were at least experimenting with stoneware compositions prior to this date.[16] Haselgrove and Murray report him being possibly assisted in initial tests for preparing suitable compositions, and perhaps in the construction of a kiln, by Johann Glauber's Philosophical Furnaces published in London 1651-52.[17] The extracts they quote from this work, while making reference to saltglaze practices, are arguably insufficiently detailed to have been of any real practical value to anyone with ambitions to manufacture the ware. If, indeed, Dwight was receiving assistance at this time it was probably provided by Robert Boyle (his old tutor at Oxford) who could claim, from amongst his several scientific achievements, a knowledge of the calcination of metals, a field that has a fundamental relevance to ceramic production. A perhaps lesser known area of Boyle's professional activities was his directorship of the East India Company. Was it as a result of this association that Dwight took up the idea of making porcelain and 'red china'? Boyle's biographical details also mention his involvement in alchemy and suggest that it *'was a logical outcome of his atomism. If every substance is merely a rearrangement of the same basic elements, transmutations should be possible.'* [18] A belief that would have been endorsed, at least in theory, by the Meissen alchemists, Böttger and Tschirnhausen.

We are provided with an insight into Dwight's approach to experimentation via the existence of a transcribed version of his recipe books.[19] Unfortunately, the originals have not been seen since the 1880s. On the basis of the evidence they provide it has been claimed that they '.... *disclose some of the patient experiments which made him a brilliant innovator, comparable with Josiah Wedgwood in the eighteenth century'.*[20] A bold statement that demands closer scrutiny. As the Wedgwood comparison poses an inappropriate diversion it is more relevant, in the present context, to examine the claim that he was a *'brilliant ceramic innovator'*.

The recipe books consist of miscellaneous details ranging from medical remedies, and the location of hidden money at the Fulham potworks, to the materials and their proportions necessary for body compositions. Dwight's notes reveal interesting details concerning the variety of materials used and practices that accompanied their preparation. An extrapolation of this information produces the following list of minerals and substances; powdered flints, white

sand, white lead, mangan (manganese), saltpetre, iron scales, ground zaffer, 'best smalt', and barillia (barilla). There is an additional preparation identified as 'White Earth' for which details are provided on page 57.[21] It reads as follows;

'To make the White Earth in a larger quantity at one time. Take first white sand sifted fine and thirty pounds Powder'd & sifted saltpeter (sic) & tartar two pounds & Half Weigh mingle and dispose of it in faulty bottles to be burnt as on ye other side.' This entry makes apparent a relatively modest list of preparations. A similar analysis of minerals etc., used by the contemporary manufacturer of delftware would prove equally numerous and varied. It is, moreover, unclear from other entries the extent to which, for example, Dwight prepared such minerals as white lead and *best smalt* himself or acquired them in a processed form from an outside source. It is, however, obvious with reference to his directions for the preparation of *'white earth'* and other ingredients that he understood and practised calcination; a procedure that he would have supposedly learnt in the laboratory of Robert Boyle. On the other hand his use of tartar and barilla was probably unusual in Britain at this period outside the practices surrounding delftware and glass production.[22] Irrespective of whether the zaffer or powdered flints were bought in, or processed at Fulham, his list of materials was not, even by seventeenth century standards, exceptional. Furthermore, there is nothing in the books to suggest the use of chemical practices that were beyond the capabilities of contemporary delftware manufacturers.

Dwight's claims to have made porcelain are also unwarranted because the term china was often used arbitarily from the sixteenth century. Hardness and whiteness were usually all that was necessary to justify a potter's belief that he had achieved success in its production. Again, with reference to Dwight's documented recipes it is easy to refute any alleged porcelain-making credentials. On page eight is entered a recipe for such a composition;

'To make transparent porcelain or China Clay
Take fine white thirty pounds
Best Clay sifted twenty pounds
Mingle and tread.'

To have achieved any degree of translucency with this body would have necessitated turning the wares to an extreme thinness. He does, indeed, go on to note; '*This Works strong & may be wrought thin upon ye wheel.*'; a point that warns against a definition of porcelain made on the basis of translucency alone. True porcelain, while usually displaying the property, is more accurately defined with reference to its ingredients. The absent mineral in the above composition is a mineral or glassy flux in the form of felspar or alternatively a ground glass substitute. Certain later Staffordshire potters, with reference to such a claim, would have been justified in calling their thin, white salt-glazed wares porcelain, especially those formed by slip casting.

Dwight's place in ceramic history is, I believe, made much more convincingly when based upon his ware's technical and aesthetic qualities. The finely thrown and turned white vessels, and magnificent portrait busts, especially those of his daughter, Lydia (V&A) and a life size bust of Prince Rupert (BM), stand out as exceptional achievements in the history of English ceramics.

Brown saltglaze wares were also produced at Nottingham from the early 1690s by James Morley, a potter identified in Dwight's lawsuit issued on the 20 June, 1693. Morley's work is less well documented than that of the plaintiff or his co-defendants, with the exception of John Chandler. The most interesting documentary evidence for Morley's products is an illustrated advertisement (Bodleian Library, Oxford) which shows four reticulated items and 'A Mogg' and 'A Decantor' which were thrown, turned but not pierced. In view of the obvious technical quality demonstrated by surviving examples it is, perhaps, surprising that only a few years earlier he was described as a brickmaker.[25] Morley's potworks, situated in Mughouse Lane (Beck Street), was continued by various members of the family until the early years of the nineteenth century. As in Staffordshire the eventual expiration of Dwight's patent allowed others to benefit from the market for saltglaze wares. A close descendant of James, a Charles Morley achieved some distinction by becoming Sherriff of Nottingham in 1737.[26]

NOTES TO CHAPTER 1

1. See Dennis Haselgrove and John Murray, 'John Dwight's Fulham Pottery 1672-1978, A Collection of Documentary Sources', *Journal of Ceramic History*, No.11 Stoke-on-Trent City Museum, 1979. Hereafter referred to as Haselgrove and Murray, Dwight.

2. Edward Vernon, son of John Vernon, and grandson of Sir Edward Vernon, Knt., of Houndshill, married Lettice, daughter of John Banks of Uttoxeter, (Staffs.) and was father of the Rev. Edward Vernon, Rector of St. George's, Bloomsbury, who died unmarried in 1765.

3. His name does not appear in the matriculation books of the university.

4. Rhoda Edwards, 'London Potters circa 1570-1710', *Journal of Ceramic History No.6*, George Street Press, Stafford, 1974, p.60.

5. G.W. Leibniz, *Samliche Werke*, Series 1, Vol. 1, pages 410 and 427.

6. L.M. Solon. Art of the Old English Potter, London, Bemrose, 1885, p.122.

7. Edwards, *Op. cit.,* p.60.

8. *Ibid,* p.60.

9. It has been suggested that both brothers moved to Bradwell in 1693 as a condition in Dwight's withdrawal of legal action against them. This arrangement would have run parallel with an agreement to dispense with Chandler's services and to supply Dwight with red clay from the site.

10. Solon, *Op. cit., p.123.*

11. Edwards, *Op. cit., p.61*

12. See 8 above.

13. *London Gazette*, No.3661, 9-12 December, 1700.

14. We do not have any contemporary documentary evidence for this event. The story has been repeated by many writers since it first appeared in *The Memoirs of George Elers*, 1902.

15. Edwards, *Op. cit.,* p.62. Although Ms Edwards recommends caution in assuming that the deceased was one and the same as the wife of John Philip, the likelihood of such a coincidence involving two women with the same name, and a German/Dutch name, is, in the author's opinion, rather improbable.

16. See Adrian Oswald, R.J.C. Hildyard and R.G. Hughes, *English Brown Stoneware 1670-1900*, London, Faber, 1982.

17. *Op. cit.,*

18. *Chambers Biographical Dictionary*, Edinburgh, 1990.

19. Haselgrove and Murray, *Dwight*, Section XVII, 'Dwight's Recipe Books 1689-1698.'

20. Oswald, *Op. cit.*, p.28.

21. Haselgrove and Murray, *Dwight*.

22. Cipriano Piccolpasso in his *Li Tre Libre Dell'arte del Vasajo*, (The Three Books of the Potter's Art) circa 1557, translated by Bernard Rackham and Albert Van der Put, London, Victoria and Albert Museum, 1934, describes the use of wine lees as a source of tartar (potassium hydrogen tartrate). It is possible that English delftware potters, especially those who used production methods based on continental practices, would have utilized the properties of tartar or a close substitute. Barilla in seventeenth century glass making is described by H. Blancourt, *Art of Glass Shewing How to make all Sorts of Glass. Crystal and Enamel.*, 1699. Reissued by Scott Greenwood London.

22. Oswald, *Op. cit*, p.102.

23. Bernard Rackham, *Catalogue of the Glaisher Collection of Pottery and Porcelain in the Fitzwilliam Museum, Cambridge*, Cambridge University Press, 1935, p.158. Hereafter referred to as Rackham, Glaisher Collection.

Top:
Slip casting with Bradwell clay.
Reconstruction 1976.
(see page 19).

Centre :
The slip-filled mould was left for approximately fifteen minutes. Slip that has not reacted with the plaster was drained away by inverting the mould. The remaining formed the vessel wall.

Bottom :
The separated mould revealing the cast form. This stage was reached after approximately one hour.

CHAPTER 2 : THE ELERS, THEIR PRODUCTS AND PRACTICES

The history of ceramic manufacture in North Staffordshire is usually described with reference to a sequence of names, events, and products which, despite variations in emphasis, follows a well established pattern. The transitional position in this chronological arrangement is invariably occupied by the Elers. Ceramic historians have, since the nineteenth century, summarised their achievement in the following terms;

'..... it was through the example of John Philip Elers .... and his brother, David Elers, that Staffordshire pottery began to rise from the level of butter pots and slipware to become an art capable of refinement'.[1]

Their work in Staffordshire attracted the attention of two distinguished contemporaries, namely Martin Lister [2] and John Houghton, both Fellows of the Royal Society.[3] The first historical references to their Bradwell Wood pottery appeared in John Aiken's *A Description of the Country from Thirty to Forty Miles Round Manchester*, 1795, and Samuel Parks', *The Chemical Catechism*, 1814. The information provided by these two sources is similar to an extent that both writers use the spelling 'Bradwall' for what is now Bradwell.[4]

Simeon Shaw, writing in the 1820s, provides a fuller account reinforced with additional details recollected by elderly inhabitants of the area who claimed, in certain instances, to have had direct links with the pottery via their antecedents. Shaw emphasises the secrecy surrounding the brothers' activities and attempts by others to obtain employment at the pottery in order to gain an insight into their production methods; a situation which has been interpreted as reflecting superior techniques and products when compared with wares from existing local concerns.

Perhaps the most significant early twentieth century addition to Shaw is provided by William Burton in his *A History and Description of English Earthenware and Stoneware.*, 1904. In view of this writer's technical knowledge, gained as a result of an impressive career with Wedgwoods and the Royal Lancastrian Pottery, it might be assumed that he was able to evaluate, for example, the Elers'

making methods; an approach that would of course have pre supposed an ability in the identification of their products. However, illustrated in this work are red stonewares that on stylistic grounds alone were made at least forty years following their departure from North Staffordshire.[5] Indeed, it was the uncertainty in making confident attributions that proved to be the greatest obstacle in arriving at an accurate assessment of the Elers' importance for ceramic developments in the district; '*It is not possible to point to a single specimen as having been made beyond doubt by the two Dutchmen*'.[6]

Although William Burton was one of the first authorities to question the validity of the Elers' transition he chose not to elaborate on his statement that '*...it is just possible that too much has been made of their doings at Bradwell Wood*'.[7] He does, however, go on to say that the Elers' importance was essentially a stimulating presence coupled with an obvious technical refinement apparent in their products, a view endorsed by later writers notably J.C. Wedgwood.[8]

The alleged Elers' involvement in salt-glazed stoneware manufacture is usually traced to their continental origins, and connections with John Dwight. Later writers, for example Arnold Mountford, believed that saltglazing was first practised in Staffordshire at a period before the circumstances outlined in Dwight's lawsuit of 1693, which was taken out against Aaron, Thomas and Richard Wedgwood, (forbears of the illustrious Josiah) and therefore quite independent of the Elers' influence.[9] In support of this view he cites evidence recorded by Shaw concerning a visit made by Enoch Wood and J. Riley to Bradwell Wood in 1808 for the purpose of examining the foundations of an oven, which in Shaw's time (the late 1820s) was '*covered by an enlargement to the barn*'.[10] It was apparently concluded by both potters that the oven was constructed for firing red stoneware only. It is here proposed that the Elers used forming methods that were not applied to white stoneware production until the late 1740s and, furthermore, that their decision not to make saltglaze wares was probably taken in the light of a settlement with John Dwight.

Simeon Shaw's most controversial addition to the Elers story involved their role in the development of an unglazed black stoneware later adapted by Josiah Wedgwood and re-named basaltes. He offers as evidence the existence of black wares in the district, mainly teapots. Despite a search through nineteenth century museum catalogues and examination of major collections, both public and private, I have failed to locate a single example of unglazed black ware in the Elers' style. Nevertheless, several writers have endorsed Shaw's account of their contribution to 'Egyptian black'. A.T. Green went as far as to offer an opinion on the quality of these phantom products;

'As in the case of the cream-coloured ware, the basalt or Egyptian black ware and the red stonewares had long been manufactured in the district, probably originating with the Elers, who produced pieces of exceptional texture and intensity of colour'.[11]

While the theory of the Elers' innovatory role in basaltes development may be traced to Shaw it has been repeated, without qualification, until recent times. I intend to argue in Chapter 3 that the manufacture of basaltes belonged to a later phase of ceramic production in Staffordshire beginning after 1750.

The best post Shaw assessment of the Elers' red stone wares is that of W.B. Honey. His selection of possible Elers' products has since been endorsed by other evidence, in particular via an examination of the brothers' production methods. His paper does not, however, make any reference to an important document in the form of a letter by Josiah Wedgwood to Thomas Bentley dated the 19 July, 1777, in which the potter outlines what he believed to be the sum total of their contribution to pottery making in North Staffordshire. It is fundamental to the current argument that Wedgwood was perceptively accurate in certain aspects of his Elers profile; a view borne out by my practical experiments, archaeological investigation, and examination of known seventeenth century stonewares. Before proceeding with an assessment of this material it is appropriate to consider their background against a wider European context.

The social and economic status of post sixteenth century ceramics was largely determined by the extent to which they were seen to reproduce the characteristics of Chinese porcelain. There were, however, two important exceptions, namely the fifteenth and sixteenth century tin-enamelled earthenwares of Spain and Italy. The maiolica istoriato pots of, for example, Faenza and Urbino are more closely related to easel paintings and engravings in their use of religious and mythological subjects, while the Hispano Moresque wares of Malaga and Valencia were dependent on decorative styles and motifs absorbed from Middle Eastern and North African sources.

With the growth in trade between the Dutch East India Company and China, during the early years of the seventeenth century, there was a corresponding increase in the use of oriental-inspired patterns on Dutch and English painted tinglaze pottery. Despite an obvious similarity in the external appearance of these products to porcelain the essential fabric of the underlying body was far removed from the translucent hardpaste composition of the Chinese originals. The earliest European attempts to imitate oriental porcelains, both Chinese and Japanese, involved the use of a glassy substitute for the mineral fluxes based on felspar.[12] These early, largely experimental wares posed troublesome technical problems that proved to be a serious deterrent to anyone except the most dedicated experimenter or wealthy patron. It is, therefore, hardly surprising that alternative experiments were undertaken involving red clays fused at stoneware temperatures. There was a Chinese precedent for effects based upon hard, opaque compositions in the form of the somewhat less well known products identified with Yixing in south eastern China. Dutch East India Company records contain several references to tablewares, mainly for the preparation and consumption of tea, that conform to surviving recognisable types. The Day Register for the Company at Batavia records from Chang Chou (in 1679) *'7 cases of red teapots'*, and in 1680 *'320 figured teapots from Macao.'* In the same year the ship 'Ternate' carried 1,635 Chinese teapots to Amsterdam.[13] The teapots in the second reference were probably red stonewares of a type known in the Netherlands as *'East Indian'* or *'Indian'* teapots, so named because they were shipped by the Company during the seventeenth century, and later, to the west via Batavia.

1. A pear shaped brown salt-glazed stoneware coffee pot which has been produced by slipcasting. This production method indicates this piece was probably made by the Elers at their Vauxhall works in London and is the only example recorded. (The spout has no strainer). Compare the lid with plate 3C.

Height 5½ ins (14 cm), c.1690. Elers probably Vauxhall, London. Courtesy Trustees the Victoria & Albert Museum.

Dwight's lawsuit of 1693 indicates that the Elers were making stoneware prior to this date. John Houghton writes in October 1693: *'There is found near Faux-hall in Surrey, a sort of clay used to make all sorts of Tea Pots ..... and lately applied to this use by two Dutch Brothers whose names are Eelers'* (Appendix 3). [Pages - 7, 9, 21, 36]

Several other ceramic pieces are known that have been enamelled in a similar way including a Chinese bowl and a London brown stoneware tankard dated 1706 (E.C.C. Trans. Vol.2, No.8, Rackham p.145) They are thought to have been painted by an imigrant Dutch glass decorator and an entry discovered by Robin Hildyard in the *'London Tradesman 1747'* refers to one such Dutchman setting up *'in the Borough'*, presumably Southwark: *'Some Years ago a Workman came over from Holland, and in a Pot-House in the Borough gave some Stone Wares the Colours common to the earthen, he succeeeded so well, that Cups and other vessels, even upon that first Essay, came little short of China-ware: But the Project was no sooner known to be in any Forwardness to become useful to the Public, than Ways and Means were found to send the Projector out of the Way, and with him the Scheme vanished.'*

2A (left). A fine quality slipcast red stoneware teapot with applied prunus sprigging. (Lid replaced).
Length 6 in. (15 cm), c.1695, Elers, probably Staffordshire. Courtesy Jonathan Horne.
Stamped into the recessed base of the teapot is an imitation Chinese seal mark (Appendix 5 fig. 1). This mark was also used on a tea kettle and an hexagonal teapot in the V&A. (Both illustrated in E.C.C. Trans Vol. 1 No.2 Plates 11B and 111A). The illustrated teapot is now in the Newcastle-under-Lyme Museum

2B (right). A small slipcast red stoneware mug decorated with an applied prunus sprig and over painted in enamels.
Height 2³/₄ ins (7 cms), c.1695, Elers, probably Staffordshire. Courtesy Jonathan Horne.
The over decoration is thought to have been executed by an immigrant glass enameller. (E.C.C. Trans. Vol. 2 No.8 Rackham p. 145). Two slipcast red stoneware teapots over decorated in a similar way are illustrated in (E.C.C. Trans Vol. 12 part 1 plate 24 and The Connoisseur Feb 1902 Solon Collection.). Compare with coffee pot, plate 1. [Page 23].

2C. A slipcast red stoneware teapot with applied stylized branches almost identical to No.3B (Lid, handle and base missing).
Height 3¹/₈ ins (7.9cms), c.1695, probably Staffordshire.
Courtesy Museum of London.
This is one of the very few examples of an Elers teapot being recovered from an archaelogical excavation. The find was made in Cowcross Street in 1989 (cow 98) adjacent to the southern end of the precinct of the Priory of the Hospital of St.John of Jerusalem, Clerkenwell, London. The teapot was in the backfill of a brick lined well (context 39 Acc No. [5]). During the 18th century this part of the site was a yard area surrounded by 'rookeries' with a very high population of usually low income families. It is therefore of some interest to find a quality teapot in this environment. Martin Lister in 1693 describes these teapots as being sold in Cheapside. (Appendix 3) which is less than one mile from where this example was found.

3A. A slipcast redware teapot and cover. The applied sprigging is almost identical to the teapot excavated in London, 2C. Height 4³/₄ ins (12cms), c.1695, Elers, probably Staffordshire.

Courtesy Sotheby's (Sale 14 July 1998).

A very similar example is illustrated in Gary Atkins' 1994 exhibition catalogue No. 43. Could these teapots be the Elers' earliest attempts at redware? The sprigging is crudely applied and they lack the quality of the other pieces in this catalogue.

3B (below, left). A fine quality slipcast red stoneware tea jar with silver mounts, (sometimes referred to as perfume bottles) each side with four different countersunk panels in the oriental style.

Height, canister 4¹/₂ ins (11.5 cms), c.1695, Elers, probably Staffordshire. Courtesy Hampshire County Museum Service.

Three other canisters are known (Macfarlane - National Art Collections Fund, Review, 1990) and if they were used as teajars they represent the first indigenous tea canisters used in this country, pre-dating the earliest tin-glazed examples. Two similar 'teajars' are known in white saltglaze, both dated '1724'. These are press moulded and although not of the same quality, may have been copied from the earlier redware examples, (Glaisher Collection No.532 and British Museum).

3C (below, right). A fine quality slipcast red stoneware teapot and cover, the sunken panels decorated in the oriental manner. Height 3⁷/₈ ins. (9.9 cms), c.1695, Elers, probably Staffordshire. Courtesy Hampshire County Museum Service.

This shape of teapot with sunken panelling probably derives from Chinese silver or porcelain. The inside has no strainer to prevent the spout becoming blocked with tealeaves. This is an early feature because in 1694 the East India Company decreed that in future any teapot made for them should always have a *'grate to be made before the spout'* (Geoffrey Godden: Oriental Export Market Porcelain, 1979 p.28). The chinoiserie panels are notably in the manner of silver. There are close similarities to a cast silver hexagonal teapot (Christie's, New York, 18 April 1989) which has a London hallmark of 1682 ('TA'). (Fully described by Margaret Macfarlane, National Art Collections Fund Review, 1990). The little lion finial is an unusual feature but is virtually the same as the one on the slipcast saltglazed-stoneware coffee-pot (plate 1). Two other similar teapots are known, one is in the Colonial Williamsburg Foundation, Virginia, and the other, in the V&A is stamped on the base with a pseudo Chinese mark Appendix 3 Fig. 1. Compare with Samuel Bell's later products, plate 15A.

4. A fine slipcast red stoneware lidded jug decorated on both sides with applied sprigs of twigs and flower motifs, the cover with flowers and flying insects.

Height 6¼ ins. (16 cms), c.1695, Elers, probably Staffordshire. Courtesy Jonathan Horne.

The handle and spout have been made from the plastic clay and have been cut and attached like metal. For a close up view see front cover. A similar example in the British Museum but with cover lacking is illustrated in Honey, E.C.C. Trans. No.2, 1934 pl.VI b. [Page 20].

5. A slipcast red stoneware teapot decorated with applied prunus sprigging. The silver gilt mounts are probably contemporary. Height 5$^1/_8$ ins. (13 cms), c.1695, Elers, probably Staffordshire. Courtesy Chipstone Foundation.

This teapot is impressed twice with a long rectangular pseudo Chinese mark (Appendix 5, Fig. 3). It is evident why in 1693 Martin Lister said that these pots "are far beyond any we have in China" (Appendix 3) and indeed are much finer than the contemporary wares being produced in Holland. Compare with (plate 9).

Two teapots in the Victoria and Albert Museum are of a different shape (ibid. Honey, plates IIb and Va). The first could be described as a tea kettle with an overhead handle. The second has vertical sides which are smoothly rounded in at the shoulder and base. Whilst most of the Elers' products were made in a light red clay the colour varied considerably, see also plates 2B and 12A. [Pages 20, 23].

6A. A straight sided red stoneware tankard, slipcast and lathe turned with applied prunus decoration.

Height 4¹/₂ in (11.5 cms), c.1695, Elers, probably Staffordshire.

Courtesy Jonathan Horne.

It is quite common for tankards at this period to be enhanced by a silver mount. A similar mug is in the British Museum (ibid. Honey, plate Ic). [Pages 30, 31].

6B. A slipcast and turned tankard with applied sprigging.

Height 6⁷/₈ ins (17.5 cms), c.1695,
probably Staffordshire,
Courtesy Norman Stretton.

The tall, slender shape of this tankard and the way the handle is applied centrally to the body displays a strong similarity to the products of other Staffordshire potters, plate 7A and Morley's early Nottingham pieces, plate 7B.

A similar tankard, but not as tall, is in the Glaisher Collection. (Ibid., Honey, plate Vb). [Pages 30, 31].

7A (top left). A thrown and turned earthenware tankard decorated with a mottled lead glaze. Height 6⅞ ins (13.5 cms), c.1700, Burslem Staffordshire. Courtesy Jonathan Horne.

Tankards and mugs of this type were being made in quantity at Burslem during the late 17th and early 18th centuries and are similar in shape to some of the Elers red stonewares, plate 6B. These utilitarian objects are rarely found today except in excavations. The use of a WR excise mark dates this piece. It became necessary for potters to mark the wares intended for the sale of liquor as proof of a correct measure. This legislation was introduced in September 1700 and at the death of the King in 1702 the Staffordshire potters started to use an AR mark. Similar tankards were also produced in brown stoneware (Staffordshire Saltglaze Stoneware, Mountford plate 5). [Pages 29, 30].

7B (middle right). A turned quart tankard in salt-glazed stoneware stamped with an AR excise mark under the handle The metallic appearance of the Nottingham glaze is very distinctive. The contemporary silver mount is inscribed 'PB 1704 RA'.
Height 6¾ ins (13cms), c.1704, James Morley, Nottingham. Courtesy Jonathan Horne.
Morley was sued by Dwight in 1693 for infringing his patent. His advertisement for stoneware produced in c.1700 (Bodlian Library) describes a similar piece as *'A Mogg'*. [Pages 7, 12, 31].

7C (below, left). A salt-glazed stoneware pint tankard produced somewhere in the London area. John Dwight of Fulham is known to have made similar tankards but so did other potters in London such as Talbot and Garner of Southwark who were sued by Dwight for infringing his patent. This tankard probably pre-dates 1700 as it has no excise mark.
Height 6 ins (12.3 cms), c.1695, London (possibly John Dwight?). Courtesy Jonathan Horne.
The Cecil Higgins Museum in Bedford has a tankard of similar turned shape in white stoneware which is probably a London piece. [Page 31].

7D (below, right). A fine turned salt-glazed stoneware tankard decorated with a white slip.
Height 6¾ ins. (17.25 cms), c.1700, probably John Dwight, Fulham, London. Courtesy Jonathan Horne.
This vessel has very pronounced turning rings on the base, and has a touch of brown slip at the top of the handle which is also under the contemporary silver mount around the rim. A feature found at Fulham is an extra piece of clay at the base of the handle which has been knife cut into a double pyramid. Chris Green has suggested that production of Dwight's 'fine white ware' which was patented in 1684 was abandoned for dipping coarser fabrics in a white slip or engobe. Great skill was needed in producing the fine wares, and costs were enormous. By the 18th century larger vessels were in demand in particular pint and quart tankards which were difficult to achieve in the fine ware. This tankard relates very closely to a white dipped coffee pot in the British Museum, (illustrated: Ars Ceramica, No.4, Hugh Tait, p.5). Few quality pieces were made at Fulham after Dwight's death in 1703.

8A. A 'butter pot' believed to have been excavated in Burslem, found during the early years of this century.

Height 13 ins (33 cms), c.1670, Staffordshire.
Courtesy Potteries Museum Stoke-on-Trent.

These tall cylindrical vessels were supplied to farmers for retailing butter in local markets. An act of parliament was introduced in 1661 to regulate their size and weight. Burslem was sometimes referred to as the *'Butter Pot Town'*. Robert Plot, describes their manufacture in his published account of 1686. [Pages 17, 23, 24, 29].

8B. Earthenware cups probably used for spirit, recovered from the A.J. Finney site at Longton, Staffordshire. They have been misfired and are therefore termed 'wasters'

Height 2½ ins (6.5 cms) each, 18thC., Longton, Staffordshire.
Courtesy the author.

Both stacks, despite being made from the same clay, show marked differences in colour, resulting from the effects of oxidation and reduction on the clay's natural iron content; the black wasters having been subjected to a greater degree of reduction. Such accidents probably led to the later manufacture of a true basaltes composition.

8C. A slipware dish, a combed slipware cup and an ironglaze cup.

Dish diameter 13 ins (33 cms), c.1690, Staffordshire.
Courtesy Potteries Museum,

Stoke-on-Trent.

These items were excavated at the Sadler site, Burslem and are representative of the types of wares being produced in North Staffordshire at the time the Elers first started production there. [Pages 17, 29, 30, 31].

The main production method used for such wares was throwing and turning followed by the application of relief decoration either by free-hand modelling or from moulds. Those wares made for tea drinking, and hence in great demand in Japan, were made in a variety of shapes that ranged from the clean-cut patterns as depicted in the work of Dutch still-life artist, van Roestraten (1630-98) to shapes based on melon, gourd, and other fruit forms. It is indicative of the public's perception of Yixing wares that some examples were mounted with silver (Plate 9A) and further ornamented with semi-precious stones. That the high values attached to these wares was not limited to European markets is reflected in a claimed documented instance of a sixteenth century Chinese official paying 500 tael for a single teapot.[14]

It was against this background that the Elers embarked on a series of events that led them to England. Whether this background included, as was later claimed by David Elers, experience of saltglaze production in Germany is uncertain. A working knowledge of stoneware firing would have certainly proved a useful qualification in connection with firing the red clay of North Staffordshire.[15]

At the time of the Elers' tenancy at Bradwell Hall existing potters in the area were using simple lead glazes for slipware, iron-glazed ware and butter pots.(Plates 8A,8C). In other parts of Britain, especially in the London area, delftwares were being produced at the highest level.[16] An objective assessment of these two categories of products makes it perfectly clear that, from a purely technical standpoint, the London-type tin-glazed pots were superior to anything from Staffordshire kilns. When viewed in this context the Elers' red stonewares take on a particular importance as representing levels of skill and, indeed, practical understanding that conceivably served as an inspiration to their Staffordshire contemporaries. It has, therefore, been traditionally assumed that they played an indirect part in the improvements to trade and ware quality that are apparent in certain post 1700 products.

The Elers brothers then recent arrival in the country and remoteness of their potworks would suggest that they were provided with details concerning the existence of suitable clays in the district. It seems probable that this information was conveyed to them either directly or indirectly by John Dwight. If, indeed, Dwight possessed any knowledge of Staffordshire's clay deposits it was probably as a result of his connections with the city of Chester. It is known from well documented sources that he held secretarial and legal appointments under four Bishops of that city, Brian Walton, Henry Ferne, George Hall and John Wilkins.[17] The appointment under Bishop Wilkins was dissolved following an allegation that Dwight had withheld documents and sums of money. Records for the baptism of his children indicate that he was residing at Wigan, where the Bishop was also rector, and that the Dwight family continued to live there until 1670/71.[18]

The obvious parallels in the work and interests of Dwight and the Elers and, indeed, the direct links resulting from the Fulham potter's lawsuits, have led to uncertainties in attributing seventeenth century red stonewares to London or Staffordshire. In addition attempts to separate Elers' red stonewares from wares of a similar type, by certain eighteenth century potters in North Staffordshire, were often devalued by confusion and uncertainty. Such uncertainties had the effect of preventing a true assessment of the Dutchmen's contribution to the development of ceramics in the region.

Old museum catalogues and labels, including those of the British and Victoria and Albert Museums, illustrate the extent and respectability of the identification problem.[19] In many instances these so-called 'Elers' wares' were made at least forty years after the brothers' departure from the area. Accordingly, certain misattributions should not have occurred their relief ornamenations being similar to those found on salt and lead-glazed products of the post 1730 period.

The attribution of Elers' ware has been made possible via the identification of their forming methods. Although I made this 'discovery' in 1975 Josiah Wedgwood committed to paper an account of the brothers' contribution to ceramic development in Staffordshire which partly corresponds with my own. He was drawn into the subject as a result of a commission from Paul Elers for a portrait medallion of his father, John Philip, (frontispiece) which, it was proposed, would carry an inscription to the effect that Elers senior was, in essence, the inventor of pottery making in Staffordshire. In a letter to his partner, Thomas Bentley, written in 1777, Wedgwood offers his estimation of the Elers' right to such an important distinction;

'The improvements Mr. Elers made in our manufactory were precisely these - glazing our common clays with salt which produc'd Pot'd Grey or stoneware, and after this they (the Elers) had left the country was improved into White Stone Ware by using the white Pipe Clay instead of the common clay of this Neighbourhood, and mixing with it Flint Stones calcin'd and reduced by pounding into a fine powder.

The next improvement introduc'd by Mr. E. was the refining of our common red clay by sifting, and making it into Tea and Coffee ware in imitation of the Chinese Red Porcelain, by casting it in plaster moulds, and turning it on the outside upon Lathes, and ornamenting it with the tea branch in relief, in imitation of the Chinese manner of ornamenting this ware - for these improvements, and very great ones they were for the time, we are indebted to the very ingenious Messrs. Elers, and I shall gladly contribute all my power to honour their memories, and transmit to posterity the knowledge of the obligations we owe them, but the sum total certainly does not amount to inventing the Art of Pottery in Britain'.[20]

Wedgwood's account was presumably based upon a personal examination of their wares plus oral evidence. A document in the Wedgwood Company archives entitled *Some Memorandums Relative to Pottery in Burslem and its Neighbourhoods*, January 2 1764 composed by Wedgwood from information recounted to him by Edward Bourne of Chesterton is similar in content to the Wedgwood/Bentley letter;

'Turning, or the use of lathes we owe to them likewise for though they either could not find a hand capable of throwing Teaware, they therefore cast their ware in plaster moulds & turn'd it on the outside very neatly in a Lathe .... It is most probable we had also the art of preparing the alabaster, makeing it into moulds & casting the ware there in from these Foreign Potters.'.

This document contains three important points, two of which conflict with the opinions of most later writers. Wedgwood's reference to lathe turning concerned an innovation which many have considered to be the Elers' principal contribution to pottery manufacture and, therefore, the least contentious part of the statement. However, the information that they were probably responsible for the introduction of plaster-of-Paris to the region is contrary to Simeon Shaw's belief that plaster was first brought to Staffordshire by Ralph Daniel, as a result of a visit to France sometime during the 1740s.[21]

If, on the other hand, there is any substance in the legendary secrecy surrounding the Dutchmen's activities at Bradwell, Shaw and the Elers' contemporaries would not have known of their use of the material despite it being widely adopted on the continent before the eighteenth century. An Italian writer of a treatise on maiolica production, Cipriano Piccolpasso (drafted circa 1557) offers a clear description of plaster moulds in connection with the pressing technique, which he recommends in instances where there is a need for items that are impossible to achieve by wheel methods.[22]

Slip casting at such an early date, before 1700, was, for such as G.W. and F.A. Rhead a much more contentious issue;

'The saltglazing is a controversial matter, but Wedgwood's statement that the Elers made ware "by casting it in plaster moulds and turning it on the outside upon lathes," is astounding. To turn cast ware upon a lathe is a feat so difficult as to be nearly impossible. And there can be no compensating advantages'.[23]

While the Rheads were experienced ceramic designers and, therefore, supposedly well versed in manufacturing principles they made the unfortunate error of evaluating Wedgwood's account in the context of late nineteenth century industrial methods.

It had been discovered as early as 1820 that the conversion of clay to a castable state was greatly facilitated by the introduction of small amounts of the alkalis sodium silicate, soda ash or some other alternative electrolyte.[24] Alkalies can separate and, in effect, lubricate the clay's molecular particles which, even in modestly plastic clays, possess a strong mutual affinity. In modern manufacture casting is often used for bodies that are too 'short'[25] for other forming processes, e.g. jollying, jiggering and pressing. Cast wares are usually fragile when pre fired and semi dried, and to an extent that, as suggested by the Rhead brothers, lathe turning would have proved difficult if not impossible. Their incredulity at Wedgwood's decription of the Elers' making process was therefore based on the wrong assumption that they were handicapped by the problems associated with turning cast forms made from chemically derived slips.

For decades prior to the discovery of deflocculents potters, including Wedgwood, had utilized the properties of liquid clay other than for its well established decorative purposes. Certain white salt-glazed stonewares and some English and continental porcelains were slipcast using water slips before 1760. That the Elers used the process is made more significant by the fact there is no evidence to suggest anyone else had formed wares by casting prior to their work at Bradwell Wood. The obvious question is why did they not throw their wares ? The answer probably has much to do with their possible inexperience in normal potting methods. As silversmiths, with a knowledge of other metal-forming procedures, they were, no doubt, familiar with workshop practices surrounding the making of pewter. Basic forms in the metal were cast, followed by turning to remove any excess metal, and to create, for example, lines and bands and to improve surface finish. It may, indeed, be significant that similar features on the Elers' red stonewares were probably inspired by pewter prototypes.

If we are to believe Shaw's story concerning the great secrecy surrounding their activities at Bradwell it is easy to appreciate why they chose not to employ local labour. Furthermore, the modest technical quality of contemporary slip-decorated and iron glaze wares suggests that it is highly unlikely there were craftsmen in the district capable of performing the high standards of manual dexterity that their stonewares, and associated working practices, demanded. The potential market for the Elers' products lay with those familiar with sophisticated wares from the Far East. The time necessary for the achievement of throwing skills appropriate to the production of forms that would provide acceptable substitutes for Yixing stonewares was, from the Elers standpoint, presumably impractical.[26]

As many untempered clays are not suitable for undeflocculated casting it follows that the red Bradwell marls were free from the problems that normally resulted from excessive plasticity. In order to gain a clearer insight into the characteristics and qualities of the material I carried out, in 1975, a series of experiments with clay from the locality. At that time the area surrounding Bradwell Hall Farm had been largely taken over for clay quarrying in connection with brick and tile manufacture, while the hall itself and outbuildings were occupied by a company known as Bradwell Industrial Aggregates. The then abundance of red marl on the site and its long history of brick and tile manufacture rendered invalid Celia Fienne's observation that 'coming to an end of their clay they made use of for that sort of ware and therefore was remov'd to some other place'.[27]

In view of the dry summer of 1975 the excavated clay was devoid of any apparent water content and to an extent that it appeared almost stone-like in texture. Normal pounding with a pestle and mortar was ineffective therefore to reduce the lumps of clay to a powdered state necessitated the use of a hammer. It proved so remarkably free from grit and vegetation that sieving was carried out merely in order to achieve even blending and a creamy consistency. The clay's most valuable property was the ease with which it formed a slip when mixed with water. In practice less than 30oz. of water converted 15oz. of clay to a castable state. These figures reveal their true significance when compared with modern casting slip recipes.[28] Some indication of gelling and drying times was established by casting the resulting body in a simple plaster-of-Paris mould. (page 14). It is relevant to mention that in connection with this stage of the process it was necessary to follow the initial filling with additional amounts of slip to compensate for the sinking which occurred as water was absorbed by the mould. Three toppings up proved to be adequate. The time between the final filling and the stage where the form could be safely removed varied according to the dryness of the plaster; some half dozen castings were usually possible. The first two forms were each in turn ready for removal within fifty minutes of the first pouring. This time was doubled with the fifth and sixth castings. If the Elers were operating with at least twelve moulds a satisfactory production rate was possible, especially in the light of the ware's market value.

Following a suitable drying period the resulting items were turned and in some cases decorative features were added in the form of reeded bands, similar to those seen on surviving Elers' products. [29]

The fine particle size of the Bradwell clay facilitated the creation of an attractive burnished surface which was preserved and even enhanced by firing. Leather hard strength was impressive and to an extent that compared favourably with products made by throwing.

My interest in their manufacturing technique preceded any knowledge of either the Wedgwood/Bentley letter of 1777 or the account of E. Bourne for initially, in line with the guidance provided by W.B. Honey, I attempted to classify possible Elers' wares on the basis of stylistic features. It is generally recognised that the banded and sprig-ornamented mugs associated with Elers and Dwight also occur in other product types, made by the Elers contemporaries, (Plates 12A/B, 13C/D), and also blanc-de-chine porcelains supplied to the East India Companies. Hanley Museum possesses three examples of red stoneware which conform to design characteristics found in Chinese porcelains made for the European market. Close examination of these pieces revealed features found only on wares formed by slip casting. The sinking in the well of the small tea bowl (page 34) and air holes in both this piece and the tankard are unquestionably a result of the use of slip pouring methods. Where pots were mounted on the lathe cone during turning, burnishing of the inner surface was clearly impossible; accordingly imperfections generally remain. Furthermore, any attempt to carry out total smoothing by spinning in, a 'chum' or clay collar would have caused scarring to the cast form's smooth outer surface. [30]

Additional red stonewares were examined in the collections of the Victoria and Albert and British Museums. In every case where a piece complied with the Eler's stylistic classification the grainy surface, sinking and air holes first seen on the Hanley pieces were in evidence. Having established that casting was practised before 1700 this single fact is unhelpful in distinguishing between Elers' wares and red stonewares that might have been made by Dwight. Trial holes dug at Bradwell Hall Farm in 1955 unearthed a number of (approximately seventy) small red stoneware fragments, all from pots made by slip casting, which also matched in quality the high standard of surface finish associated with extant wares of the Elers' type. Without exception all the seventeenth century wares examined were slipcast.

It is necessary to consider the possibility that the technique was also practised at Fulham by John Dwight. Excavations undertaken by the Fulham and Hammersmith Historical Society on the site of the Fulham Pottery, as might be expected, unearthed large quantities of brown salt-glazed stoneware. The few fragments of red stoneware recovered are significantly coarser than any of the finely potted vessels identified as Elers in museum collections, and, perhaps more importantly, bear features attributable to throwing; no wasters from slipcast wares were found. [31] (Plate 14A).

In addition to excavated evidence there is proof of Dwight's methods in a hand-written document found in the 19th century among some account books at the Fulham Pottery. He records the following recipe for a stoneware body made from Staffordshire red clay; 'To make a bright red clay with Staffordshire red clay; *'Take sifted Staffordshire Clay thirty pounds ffine dark twenty pounds, mingle and tread'*.[32] Dwight's instructions *'mingle and tread'* are crucial to an understanding of his making procedure for it was necessary to carry out the kneading stage as a preliminary to throwing or pressing. The Elers use of casting would of course have avoided the need to return the slip to a plastic state. If Dwight's recipe book, and the wares excavated at Fulham are, indeed, representative of the pottery's output it follows that the surviving seventeenth century fine red stonewares showing characteristics inconsistent with his manufacturing technique were made elsewhere; in all probability by the Elers.

The former attribution problems were outlined by Bernard Rackham;

'There is less doubt as to the wares they (the Elers), made. A fair number of pieces survive, in hard unglazed ware ranging in colour from brick red to chocolate brown (Plates 4, 5 and 12) which on chronological grounds could be attributed to them, but the difficulty is to distinguish their productions from the opaceous red and dark-coloured porcelain or china for which Dwight obtained a patent in 1684; nor is it possible to surmise which of the pieces that may be conjecturally accepted as their work were made at Fulham and which after their removal northward. A division of material is not practicable, since Dwight and presumably the Elers brothers obtained clay from Staffordshire for the wares they made at Fulham'.[33]

Whilst the separation of Elers' wares from the red wares manufactured by Dwight may be made on the basis of technique any attempt to differentiate between the Elers' Vauxhall wares from those made at Bradwell does not appear possible, (except perhaps Plate I) especially if they were working with Staffordshire clays prior to moving to the area. On this point the situation is unchanged from the time when Rackham expressed an opinion on the subject.

It is known from evidence provided by both extant specimens and excavated wasters from the Bradwell site that casting was also used in the forming of teapot lids and spouts. Handles for mugs and teapots were on the other hand, made from clay in its plastic state. There are important practical considerations that account for these differences in procedure. Cast rods or strips would, for example, have been considerably weaker than comparable items made from plastic clay carefully prepared by kneading or wedging. It was, therefore, usual practice to make handles from strips of clay which could be bent to correspond with the vessel's contours. Furthermore, the almost machine-like precision of the Elers' handles, and the fineness and accurate arrangement of raised bands on their mugs, suggests the use of carefully prepared metal profiles for this purpose.

As John Dwight applied decorative reliefs to his salt-glazed stonewares it needs to be considered whether these same subjects might also occur on red wares from his pottery. Miss Mavis Bimson examined the possibility of such a relationship in a paper read to the English Ceramic Circle. She concludes; *'Up to the present time no "red porcelain" has been found bearing applied decoration identical with that on the salt-glazed stoneware. Without this type of evidence the identification of Dwight's "red porcelain" is not possible'.*[34] Miss Bimson's investigation also included the 'red porcelain' held by the British Museum which I saw in 1975 and identified as the products of slip casting. Accordingly it seems reasonable to conclude that all surviving pieces of this type were made by the Elers in London and Staffordshire.

The fineness and sharpness of detail evident in the Elers' relief ornamentations is attributable to their use of metal dies, probably of brass. The slight roughness surrounding the die-formed details has given rise to the theory that they were formed by impressing small pads of clay attached to the vessel wall. In practice such a technique would almost inevitably have caused distortion or irreperable damage because sharp detail could not have been achieved by light pressure alone. A much more satisfactory outcome would have probably resulted from pressing clay into the mould, smoothing off on the back to remove excess clay followed by application to the wetted pot surface. In other words initial contact was achieved without separating the relief from its mould. Final finishing would have been carried out with a metal or wooden modelling tool. (detail front cover).

The development of finer stonewares such as basaltes and jasper, during the 1770s, was in fact, made possible by the introduction of a more flexible technique that involved removing the clay sprig from a porous mould (invariably of earthenware); a procedure that would have proved almost impossible if attempted with a die cast from metal.[35]

On the evidence of Celia Fiennes' diary entry the Elers had left Bradwell before 1699. It is unlikely operations were cut short by any single factor. The isolation of the hall was undoubtedly a major handicap in transporting fragile products to suitable retail outlets, and the very nature of the casting process imposed restrictions on output, which in turn increased production costs. Irrespective of the precise cause of their departure from North Staffordshire the brothers' bankruptcy was recorded in the *London Gazette* for the 2-5. December, 1700.

NOTES FOR CHAPTER 2

1. Honey, *Elers' Ware.*

2. See Appendix 3

3. See Appendix 3

4. Prior to the nineteenth century Bradwell was identified on maps and in documentary sources as 'Bradwall'.(see Plot's 1686 map of Staffordshire-inside back cover)

5. William Burton, *A History and Description of English Earthenware and Stoneware*, London, Cassell & Co., 1904, figs.21 & 22.

6. B. Rackham and H. Read, *English Pottery,* London, Ernest Benn, 1924, p.86.

7. Burton, Op. cit.

8. Wedgwood, *Staffordshire Pottery*, p.43; *'It was the refined taste and precision of execution - and the proof that it paid financially which taught the Staffordsire potters the most valuable lesson.'*

9. A.R. Mountford. *Staffordshire Salt-glazed Stoneware,*. London. Barrie & Jenkins, 1971. Hereafter referred to as Mountford, Staffordshire Saltglaze.

10. Shaw, *Staffordshire Potteries*, p.121

11. A.T. Green, "The Contribution of Josiah Wedgwood to the Technical Side of the Pottery Industry", *Ceramic Society Transactions*, Vol. XXIX, 1930.

12. The Medici workshop, Chantilly and St. Cloud produced soft-paste porcelains incorporating glassy frits; an approach to the creation of translucent compositions that was eventually taken up in Britain, initially at Chelsea.

13. D.F. Lunsingh Scheurleer, *Chinese Export Porcelain*, 1974, p.167.

14. *Ibid,* p.167.

15. The highest fired German saltglaze wares were probably exposed to temperatures in excess of 1200 degrees centigrade.

16. See Edwards, *London Potters.*

17. For further information regarding Dwight's links with Chester see Mavis Bimson, "John Dwight", *English Ceramic Circle Transactions*, Vol. V, Part 2, 1961, pp.95-109. Hereafter referred to as Bimson, Dwight.

18. See Haselgrove and Murray, *Dwight.*

19. Museum catalogues showing misattribution of Elers' and related wares; Hobson, British Museum, Bernard Rackham, Catalogue of the Glaisher Collection of Pottery and Porcelain in the Fitzwilliam Museum, Cambridge, Cambridge University Press, 1935. Hereafter referred to as Rackham, Glaisher Collection. This author, on plate 43D, illustrates a proven Elers' mug which he attributes to 1795 (possibly a printer's error) and describes it as wheel thrown.

20. Finer and Savage, *Wedgwood Letters*, pp.206-207.

21. Shaw, *Staffordshire Potteries*, p.163.

22. Cipriano Piccolpasso, *Li Tre Libre Dell'arte del Vasajo* (The Three Books of the Potter's Art) translated by Bernard Rackham and Albert Van der Put, London, Victoria and Albert Museum, 1934.

23. Rhead, *Staffordshire Pots and Potters*, p.164.

24. See A.E. Dodd, "Notes on the Early Use of Plaster and Slip Casting" *Journal of the British Ceramic Society,* Vol.6, 1969.

25. A term used to identify a clay body in which plasticity falls below a consistency appropriate to modelling and throwing.

26. Someone might conceivably use the argument that slip casting was preferred in instances where there was a requirement for thin, hence lightweight forms. This might well have been the case in connection with the later cast saltglaze wares of the 1740s. My claim that the Elers cast wares, for the reasons argued, is substantiated by the existence of Dwight and Morley thrown forms of a high quality.

27. G.C. Morris, *The Journeys of Celia Fiennes,* 1947.

28. The chemistry pertaining to casting slips is covered in several technical publications issued for the benefit of chemists employed in the ceramic industry e.g. A Heath, *A Handbook of Ceramic Calculations*, Stoke-on-Trent, Webberley, 1937.

29. In an unheated environment, and depending on air temperature, the cast forms would have been ready for turning in from two to seven days.

30. The word chum is used to identify a cylinder-shaped thrown form, used in an unfired and damp state during the process of turning wares on a potter's wheel. Depending on size and shape the item being turned is positioned over or inside the chum to facilitate the formation of a footring.

31. Dating from the 1673-75 phase suggests these pieces were experimental rather than a commercial production. They also represent the earliest English ceramic teawares yet found.

32. See facsimile of Dwight's *Commonplace Book* in Haselgrove and Murray, *Dwight.*

33. Rackham, *Staffordshire Pottery*, p.15.

34. Bimson, *Dwight.*

35. The benefits introduced by the use of 'pitcher' moulds are described in a letter from Wedgwood to Bentley dated 23 May, 1777. See E.J. Morton, *Letters of Josiah Wedgwood 1771-1780*, Manchester, E.J. Morton Publishers, 1903, pp.362-363.

CHAPTER 3 : THE ELERS AND EGYPTIAN BLACK

Starting with Simeon Shaw several ceramic historians have commented on the origins of Egyptian black by tracing its introduction to the Elers.[1] Inconsistent with this information is the fact that there are no extant black stonewares that could conceivably predate circa 1740. A matter of considerable significance concerns earlier writers' perceptions of black. Perhaps the most satisfactory reference point is the colour of post 1770 true basaltes, for in this instance there can be no doubts as to the potter's intentions. Although there exist, for example, Elers' wares that are a deep chocolate brown (Plates 2B, 5 & 12) one would not be justified in calling them black. It is also necessary to draw a distinction between a conscious attempt to make a black body and effects that resulted from a partially controlled aspect of firing; it being a well established principle that a body containing appreciable proportions of iron (ten per cent plus) will differ in ultimate effect in proportion to degrees of atmospheric reduction.

Excavated wasters from sites in North Staffordshire include items rejected because they were accidentally over reduced to produce a body that is vitrified, and darker in colour than an identical item fired under predominantly oxydising conditions. If such pieces were unrepresentative of the norm it then follows they were not what was ideally expected. It must, therefore, be concluded that any requirement for a black composition consisting of a combination of a clay and iron (where the iron content was less than ten per cent and the firing was mainly reducing) was overdependent on chance. Had the Elers attempted to produce a true basaltes then a procedure involving an iron stain (in excess of fifteen per cent) introduced to the Bradwell clay, would have led to more consistent and predictable results. Under these circumstances the chemical state of the iron stain was of considerable importance. If introduced in the form of ferrous oxide (FeO) and in amounts in excess of thirty five per cent, the use of reducing conditions was desirable but not essential.

Could it be that these dark red wares were at the root of the long-established belief that the Elers introduced basaltes or Egyptian black to the region? It has to be said at the outset that there is evidence of confusion in Shaw's comments on this subject, especially with regard to what he meant by the term *'Egyptian black'*. The following extract from his *History of the Staffordshire Potteries*, 1829, also reveals a problematic chronology;

'At this time were also made the first attempts at the ware we now call Egyptian Black; by employing the black clay only for jugs and teapots; which being rich with basaltes, and saturated with oxide of iron, became very black when fired. Several specimens are ornamented with figures, in other clays, of leaves and fruit; and a small white teapot has these in black clay. Some of the black teapots are glazed, but not all; and the stouking branch seems improved in all the specimens. In 1820, very near the front of the Burslem Free School, at a depth of almost ten feet beneath the surface of the then existing highways, which were being lowered for public convenience, were found two Butter Pots, of 1645, and several other specimens of early pottery, and which had been filled up with refuse articles. One is a jet black teapot, globose in shape, with three mole feet on the bottom, evidently of clay with some manganese, and finely glazed with lead ore; the spout, handle, and feet fixed in a superior manner'.[2]

This is a good example of Shaw's capacity for confusing the reader because the wares he identifies amount to four distinctly different product types.(Plates 8A, 16C). Furthermore, unless he is describing a butter pot that is considerably later than those seen by Plot the implication that the teawares mentioned in this passage were approximately contemporary with it is to say the least misleading.[3] Product types recovered may be further divided into three separate groups; a black ware either glazed or dry body, wares consisting of a white body ornamented with reliefs in black, and a black earthenware covered with a lead glaze which he mentions in connection with a discovery made under the pavement outside the Burslem Free

School. The wares with coloured reliefs are no longer identified within Shaw's classification, nor, indeed, are the pots which he describes as being coated with a black glaze. The first mentioned products are now labelled Whieldon/Wedgwood or Astbury type while the wares with a black glaze were, towards the end of the nineteenth century, given the rather misleading name of 'Jackfield type'; a term that should be limited to certain well defined products from the late eighteenth century made at Jackfield in Shropshire.

Shaw describes the occurrence of Egyptian black wares in the same layer as 'two Butter Pots of 1643' with the inference that they were from the same period. On stylistic grounds alone it is beyond dispute that the teapot was made at a date almost a century later than the associated finds. Reference to the 'mole feet' may be equated with the above mentioned 'Jackfield type' wares of black glazed earthenware made by Whieldon and other Staffordshire potters between circa 1735 and 1750. Any disturbance of the ground at a date prior to the above discovery could have adulterated the earlier deposits with wasters from a later period, a situation that led to this writer's erroneous attribution.

Later writers have generally accepted without question Shaw's information concerning the long history of Egyptian black production, including its claimed origins with the Elers, although it must be acknowledged that M.H. Grant was prepared to challenge his woolly terminology as early as 1910.[3] In quoting from Shaw he did however, endorse the story that a potter named Richard Lawton passed on to Wedgwood a recipe for basaltes handed down by his father, *Thomas Lawton who made for these gentlemen the first slip for Egyptian Black, and was well acquainted with the method of making the slip for the Red Porcelain, made by the Elers, at Bradwell, many years before'.*[4] He goes on to claim that;

'Old T.L. (Thomas Lawton) *being intimate with an old man named Bourne, a bricklayer resident at Chesterton, near to Bradwell, obtained from him many teapots, Red and Black, dry body, without any kind of glaze, made by the Elers, and preserved by the oldest families of the place; and the specimens, T. Lawton learned further, and informed Messrs. Wedgwood and Bentley, that Elers used only the red clay of Bradwell, and the ochre from near Chesterton, for their Pottery, and he likewise had some of the materials brought, which were properly weighed by Daniel Greatbatch, one of the foremen, and after being prepared as clay by T. Lawton, were made into articles which suggested their Black Egyptian'.*[5]

There is clearly an important difference between what Shaw understood to be Egyptian black and the ware that Grant and later historians identified with the term.

It has been shown that there is a body of archaeological, documentary and technical evidence which confirms the Elers' use of slipcasting. Significantly, casting is difficult to perform in connection with black compositions containing a high proportion of iron oxide, even with the otherwise versatile clay from Bradwell Wood.[6] After nearly two centuries of accumulated expertise the formulation of a trouble-free black casting slip is still no easy matter.

Although Shaw refers to '*many teapots, Red and Black, dry body, without any kind of glaze, made by the Elers, and preserved by the oldest families of the place,'* the existence of the second ware type mentioned has yet to be proved. In Hanley Museum there are two teapots that have been conjecturally identified during and since the nineteenth century with the potter, Joshua Twyford; an association that probably originated in an attribution made, according to L.M. Solon, by Enoch Wood in whose collection they belonged prior to being deposited with the Burslem Museum, then housed in the Wedgwood Institute.[7 and 8] (Plate 15D).

As Wood's labels that originally accompanied these pots have not survived it is impossible to ascertain the grounds for this attribution.[9] A comparison of the relief ornamentations on the bag shaped teapot with wasters from Whieldon's Fenton Vivian site has established a close similarity in the details of their moulded reliefs. Therefore, contrary to Wood's information it now seems more probable that these teapots were products of Whieldon's potworks and made at a date between 1755 and 1760. On technical and stylistic grounds one can discount the possibility of any connection with the Elers. The Twyford link was, of course, important to those who believed that the Dutchmen introduced Egyptian black or basaltes to North Staffordshire, especially in its claimed substantiation of the Astbury/Twyford working knowledge of the Elers' production process.

It is on the questionable significance of the evidence provided by the two Hanley Museum teapots, and the wares reputedly seen by Shaw and his contemporaries, now mysteriously disappeared, if, indeed, they ever existed, that the theory of the Elers/Egyptian black link was established. The absence of any black pieces in the style of identifiable Elers' red stonewares must inevitably undermine the belief that they were responsible for introducing proto basaltes to North Staffordshire. As their known wares were slip-cast it is significant that both Hanley Museum teapots were wheel thrown and finished by turning and burnishing.

In addition to the services of Thomas Lawton, Shaw describes the assistance provided by Daniel Greatbach in the preparation of Egyptian black for Wedgwood and Bentley.[10] This statement implies a level of technical knowledge that was dependent on a specialist understanding of the weighing out, mixing and perhaps firing of the black body, in effect in an area that Wedgwood himself was unable to bring to the subject. It has to be decided whether Shaw was justified in this belief.

The use of iron compounds in bodies and glazes has a long history in North Staffordshire.[11] It may have been important for the invention of black basaltes that the so-called Jackfield wares predate Josiah Wedgwood's experiments by almost twenty years. There were, therefore, in existence by the middle years of the eighteenth century well established practices involving iron-stained bodies and glazes. As there is abundant evidence of Thomas Whieldon's involvement in the production of pottery with black glazes, before and during his partnership with Wedgwood, it follows that preparing materials for these wares was part day-to-day duties at his pottery. Whieldon has recorded in a notebook, preserved in the archives of Hanley Museum, an interesting recipe;

'for black
2 pounds magnus
6 pounds ocre (sic)
2 pounds scals (sic)
3 pounds red clay

2 pounds tough tom
4 1/2 pounds white clay
1/2 pound flint'

Unfortunately, there is no mention of firing details or whether the body was formulated to receive a glaze. Excavations on the Fenton Vivian site have uncovered evidence which suggests that a basaltes composition was being made in the same context as lead and salt-glazed wares, and at a period some ten years before the appearance of the first neo-classical forms that later defined the composition.[12] A particularly interesting find from the same excavation occurred in the form of a small, overfired basaltes medallion; (Plate 16B) stylistically anticipating Wedgwood's later productions in both the black body and jasper. This item is arguably representative of the earliest experiments with cameo subjects in basaltes.

Effects obtainable with iron would have been easily determined by prior experiment. In practice it was, no doubt, found that in order to produce a good black body amounts in excess of thirty per cent were necessary. Details in Wedgwood's *Commonplace Books* and recipes published in the nineteenth century recommend additions of up to fifty per cent stain consisting of the oxides of iron and manganese.[13] An experienced potter could, almost without recourse to the preparation of test pieces, have predicted the effects of differing amounts of these oxides. Indeed, to someone of Wedgwood's experience the creation of a black body would have been a relatively uncomplicated matter. Therefore, Shaw's view that he was forced to draw on the services of Thomas Lawton and Daniel Greatbach exaggerates the scale of the challenge. Success in firing the body was, however, less predictable. A letter from Wedgwood to Bentley, dated the '*3rd, of April 1771*' provides an insight into some of the difficulties experienced.[14]

Despite the claim that an unglazed black stoneware had been in production since the time of the Elers' occupation of Bradwell Hall, evidence in the form of pre Neo-classical wares in the body is limited to the two teapots traditionally associated with Joshua Twyford, and a third which has recently been identified. (Plate 16A). These 'experimental' blackware pieces were in all probability made by Whieldon and

Wedgwood, or were the work of Wedgwood alone during the early years (from 1759) of his Burslem period.

While there is no documentary evidence that he ever made an unambiguous claim for a pre-eminent role in the invention of basaltes there is an interesting reference to its rarity in a letter to Bentley written on the 17 September, 1769;

'I want to talk very seriously to my Dear Friend about Encaustic Vases, pray sit down, take a pipe, and compose your self. If our potters once make the black body they will mimick the painting as soon as they see it' [15] (Plate 16D).

In this instance it is explicit in the words *'If our potters once make the black body'* that Wedgwood was either referring to the quality of the composition or his monopoly of it. In connection with the development of polychrome decoration, applied in the form of low gloss enamels, the reference to *'Encaustic Vases'* marks the appearance of a new technique for which he took out a patent in 1769.[16] Despite the patent Wedgwood was aware by the early summer of 1770 that his decorating technique was being copied by a neighbour, namely Humphrey Palmer of Hanley Green, who was openly retailing the goods through London china merchant, and Palmer's partner, James Neale. The following extract from a further letter to Bentley dated the 13 October, 1770 outlines Wedgwood's plans for obtaining incriminating evidence that he hoped would lead to a successful course of action;

'I expect no less than you have wrote me respecting the invasion of our Patent, and I apprehend they will persist in it to the utmost so that a tryal seems inevitable, and if so, the sooner the better. I shall therefore now just mention what upon the subject, and what Mr. Sparrow advises, as I have mentioned it to him.

I think we shall stand a much better chance to have it tryed in London than in the Country, and shall more easily prove the invasion of the Patent against Neale and Palmer, the first thing, therefore, we should do in my opinion should be to purchase a teapot from Neale, and afterwards to leave an attested copy of the Patent with him by some person who can evidence it for us. This should be done immediately as I must have the Patent sent me here that I may deliver another to Palmer. May not this affair furnish us with a good excuse for advertising away at a great rate, pray consider of this and favour me with your thought upon it'.[17]

He, perhaps, reached the conclusion that the trouble and expense in maintaining an encaustic monopoly was of questionable value. Ironically, doubts that proved to be justified for very few of his competitors went on to practise encaustic painting on basaltes.

Those who question the credibility of Shaw's methodology would find justification for their view with reference to his account of the Wedgwood/Palmer dispute;

'Being very useful for Busts, etc., Mr Josiah Wedgwood prepared it of a superior manner in grain, and blacker in colour; and obtained a patent for its entire application. His numerous beautiful productions of his body remain unrivalled. But the patent was given up, inconsequence of Mr. Palmer, of Hanley, satisfactorily proving that the articles had been used some time before Mr. Wedgwood commenced business'. [18]

In conclusion, Shaw was, of course, wrong in believing that the disagreement was based on conflicting claims concerning the origins of the basaltes body; a situation which inevitably led to the misinterpretation, among some early ceramic historians, that Wedgwood's failure to maintain patent protection was due to a long tradition of Egyptian black production in North Staffordshire, dating back to the Elers. It is much more likely that because iron had been used in connection with certain bodies and glazes since the seventeenth century he would have probably felt unjustified in claiming a unique role as the inventor of basaltes. Nevertheless, if we accept the evidence provided by the wasters from Fenton Vivian, and their close similarity to the relief ornamentations on the 'Twyford' teapot, and the pots illustrated, (Plates 15C,D, 16A) it is clear that the partners were making basaltes before 1760, if only on an experimental basis.

Unless the Elers' dark red stonewares were misleadingly described as black there are no grounds for suggesting the existence of a truly black composition before circa 1758.[19] It has been argued that in instances where this darkening of the fired body occurred the effect was due to the presence of reducing conditions that were probably not intended. It is, moreover, important that we differentiate between these accidental effects and the formulation of a black body in which the colour resulted from a high proportion (perhaps as much as fifty per cent) of artificially introduced iron and manganese oxides. The 'Twyford' teapot is a product of such a procedure.

NOTES TO CHAPTER 3

1. Typically L.M. Solon, *The Art Of The Old English Potter*, London, Bemrose, 1885 and G.W and F.A. Rhead, *Staffordshire Pots and Potters*, London, Hutchinson, 1906.

2. Shaw, Page 123.

3. M.H. Grant, *The Makers of Black Basaltes*, 1910.

4. Shaw, *Staffordshire Potteries*, p.187.

5. *Ibid*, p.187-188.

6. The casting of a traditional basaltes composition, with its high proportions of iron and manganese oxides is not possible in conjunction with alkaline materials e.g. soda ash and sodium silicate. The deflocculating properties of these chemicals act on the clay content of the body which, in the case of basaltes, was often below fifty per cent.

7. There is no evidence to indicate the precise nature of Joshua Twyford's ceramic output. J.C. Wedgwood, Staffordshire Pottery and Its History, London, 1913, makes reference to a list 'of those who joined the "Association to defend and avenge King William" in 1696 ..... preserved at the Record Office (presumably William Salt Library, Stafford). Among 100 names given in Stoke-on-Trent, which included Hanley, Shelton. Longton & c, occur side by side the names of 'Joshua Twiford' and 'Robert Astbry'. Is it now possible that even then they had their pot-banks side by side, as tradition says, on the knoll where Shelton Church now stands. In attributing the so-called 'Twyford teapot' to this potter it was assumed that he had gained a knowledge of basaltes manufacture as a result of his alleged employment by the Elers, (See Shaw, *Staffordshire Potteries*, p.119). Twyford's potworks was reputedly located in Shelton, Stoke-on-Trent, on the hill near the recently excavated Shelton Farm site. This same teapot was also identified as a product of John and Thomas Wedgwood. See note 9.

8. 'They were presented by Enoch Wood, who knew them to be the work of Twyford (one of their imitators), as the label attached to the pieces and written in his own hand testifies.' Solon, *Art of the Old English Potter*, p.129. Although Solon recorded this information before 1885 (the publication date of the *Art of The Old English Potter*) Wood's label was then at least forty-five years old, if in fact it was written by Enoch Wood; he died in 1840.

9. Diana Edwards, *Black Basalt Wedgwood and Contemporary Manufacturers*, Woodbridge, Antique Collectors' Club, 1994, p.26 states: 'Contrary to popular opinion, Wedgwood was not the first to manufacture the black basalt body in England; eventually more than 150 potteries were in this arena'. In support of this view is cited annotations by Enoch Wood in a copy of William Pitt's *Topographical History of Staffordshire*, 1817, p.416, which attribute the 'Twyford teapot' and the other early basaltes teapot to John and Thomas Wedgwood of Burslem. This information is of course contrary to the attributions reported by Solon which also originated, we are told, with Enoch Wood. In view of these apparent contradictions I also examined the photocopies of Pitt's work in the Stoke-on-Trent City Museum. The complete annotation reads as follows; '*This Egyptian Black Clay, which Wedgwood took out a patent to use exclusively. Palmer of Hanley proved it was not New & voided this Patent. Thos. & John Wedgwood who built the Big House made this Black Ware but Jos Wedgwood made it of a blacker hugh & introduced it of superior Quality in both form and Colour. I have the Original specimens (made by Thos. & John Wedgwood before the Big House in Burslem was built by them) in my Museum*'. Like Shaw Enoch Wood was mistaken in claiming that Wedgwood had attempted to patent basaltes. His 1769 patent was in fact taken out to protect the enamel (encaustic) painting technique and not the underlying body. I would offer the following points as also being incompatable with Wood's claim;

(1). If, as Wood suggests, the teapots predate the

existence of the Big House they would have had to have been made before 1750, while stylistically they belong to the post 1750 period.

(2). If they were made by J & T Wedgwood why did they not go on to make basaltes wares in the Neo-classical style?

Thomas Wedgwood's dates are 1703-76, and John Wedgwood's 1705-80. Their sales account book indicates that John was potting up to his death in 1780. See Mountford, Staffordshire Saltglaze, p.21.

(3). Wood attributed them to a period before his birth (1759) thereby indicating a dependance on handed-down information.

(4). He is known to have made mistakes in connection with other attributions.

(5) His annotations reveal a degree of unfavourable opinion, even bias, towards Josiah Wedgwood.

10. Shaw, *Staffordshire Potteries*, p.188.

11. The colouring properties of iron oxide, for producing black glazes, were applied to the production of the so-called 'cistercian' wares in Staffordshire before 1650.

12. A.R. Mountford, "Thomas Whieldon's Manufactory at Fenton Vivian," *Transactions of the English Ceramic Circle.* Vol.8. Part 2. 1972, pp.164-182.

13. Typically William Evans, *Art and History of the Potting Business*, Shelton, 1846, and *Recipes for Enamel, Underglaze, and Majolica Colours and Lustres*, London, Smith Greenwood, undated.

14. *'We drew a biscuit kiln of very good vases on Monday, nearly all black ones, with some Teapots ...... We have not fired quite so hard this time. I had ordered them to be a little easier on account of the feet being crooked, and other accidents attending a hot fire; but I find nevertheless many of the feet warped, though they the men who place them in the oven-assure me the vases were set as they knew how ...... There is a way in which I believe they may be made with slender yet straight feet, and that is to make them separate, and afterwards fix the vase, foot and plinth*

together by a pin, screw and nut ...... There are objections to this method, but as we must fire our Vases till they become almost glass, and are therefore in a very soft state in the oven, I do not know any other method of preventing or having crooked footed ones.' Finer and Savage, Wedgwood Letters, pp.104-105.

15. *Ibid*, p.79.

16. See *Appendix 4* for a synopsis of Wedgwood's encaustic patent.

17. Finer and Savage, *Wedgwood Letters*, pp.98-99.

18. Shaw, *Staffordshire Potteries*, p.124.

19. In this instance the truly black composition to which I refer was a body that was unglazed in its completed state.

CHAPTER 4 : THE ELERS' STAFFORDSHIRE CONTEMPORARIES

Given the previous uncertainty in attributing wares to the Elers their reputation clearly owed more to traditional belief than ascertainable fact. It is, perhaps, immaterial that pieces thought to be by them were often from a period forty or more years after the abandonment of their Bradwell pottery. That they were perceived to be capable of such standards is in itself a measure of the esteem in which they were held since the eighteenth century. Their foreignness and claimed social status also set them apart from the indigenous population. Any assessment of the Elers' importance must, therefore, take the form of an objective comparison between what they are known to have made, and those wares already being produced in Staffordshire at the time of their arrival in 1693.

Archaeological and documentary evidence for the post 1680 period reveals a situation in which the greatest concentration of potters was located in Burslem. Dr. Robert Plot in his *Natural History of Staffordshire* 1686, reports;

'The greatest pottery they have in this County, is carried on at Burslem, near Newcastle-under-Lyme, where for making their several sorts of Pots, they have as many different sorts of Clay, which they dig round about the Towne'.[1]

He goes on to identify four easily recognisable product types *'black wares', 'yellow-coloured ware'*, wares of a *'Motley colour, which is procured by blending the Lead with Manganese'* and *'Butter-pots'*. The black pots, now identified as being glazed with a combination of lead and iron, constituted the longest established type by the 1690s. Excavations in Burslem and chance discoveries provide a clear picture of their co-production alongside butter pots and the first slipwares.[2]

Writers on English medieval pottery, notably Bernard Rackham, suggested that the earliest examples belong to the late medieval phase; in other words just prior to Henry VIII's Dissolution of the monasteries.[3] The monastic connection and hence the term 'cistercian ware' arises from the discovery of ironglaze fragments on abbey sites in Yorkshire, in particular Fountains. It is,

however, far from certain thay they date from the abbey's occupation. Indeed, there is evidence to suggest that in many instances others moved on to these sites to exploit the high quality materials that could be salvaged by demolishing existing structures. In some cases actual occupation occurred, which possibly continued for several generations.[4] The Burslem material would appear to date from the 1640s, at the earliest, and accordingly represents the first stage in an unbroken tradition of pottery making in the area.

The most significant technical aspect of these wares is that they identify the potter's use of iron as a glaze colourant. That there was, nevertheless, some uncertainty concerning the precise amount of iron necessary for optimum effect is evident in the existence of glazes where the oxide was excessive, hence dry effects resulting from saturated solutions.[5] The butter pots, also mentioned by Plot, were made according to similar procedures and with identical materials. Glaze quality, especially the requirement for a decorative shiny black effect, sought in connection with tygs and other small vessels, does not appear to have been a priority. The most persistent problem, leading to actual losses, is attributable to the creation of fire cracks and glaze sulphurization due in the latter case to an inadequate supply of oxygen during the single biscuit/glost firing.

It is, perhaps, to be expected that stratified sites generally reveal a chronological sequence in which iron-glazed items appear at an earlier date than slipwares. There are, however, instances where both product types were being made at the same time. We are fortunate in having material excavated from Burslem that is approximately contemporary with the Elers' work at Bradwell Wood. Stoke-on Trent City Museum was in the mid 1950s involved in a rescue excavation on a site then and, indeed, still occupied by the firm of John Sadler. The material recovered consisted of iron glaze, slipwares and mottled wares; in all probability the products of a single pottery operating during the period from circa 1680 to 1700. (Plate 8C). The finds may be evaluated in two ways (a) their technical significance and (b) an estimation of the potter's approach to quality control indicated by what was discarded, and therefore unearthed by the excavation.

The materials used, especially in the choice of clays for slip decoration, were based upon what I identify as an opportunistic approach to production.[6] In other words the slips were characterised by the presence of ingredients that were not added by the potter. In the 17th century Plot reports that the clays he saw consisted of a *Bottle Clay, of a bright whitish colour, and fuller intersperst with a dark yellow, which they use for their black wares, being mixt with the Red Blending Clay, which is a dirty red colour. White Clay, so called it seems though blewish colour, and used for making yellow-coloured ware, because yellow is the lightest colour they make any Ware of*[7] The opposite of opportunism is prescription where bodies, colours and glazes are made up from different materials combined to produce a specific effect, a procedure associated with the more technically sophisticated areas of ceramic production, for example, delftware and porcelain. Slipwares, moreover, occupied a midway point in the market structure between delftware and the coarse lead glazed storage jars and cooking pots also made in Staffordshire and at numerous rural workshops. The position of slipwares in this market structure is important in arriving at an evaluation of wares attributed to the Elers, given that they represent the Burslem potter's most technically significant achievement before circa 1700.

It has already been claimed that in examining what the potter rejected we are able to arrive at an assessment of his approach to quality control. The Sadler finds reveal problems arising from fire cracks and warping, being especially prevalent amongst flat wares. The glaze faults seen amongst iron-glazed wares were rare on slipwares, indeed most examples from this excavation have a good glossy surface.

The third ware type found here, and on other late seventeenth century Staffordshire sites, is characterised by a mottled brown glaze (Plate 7A) and the use of turned bands similar to those found on Elers' red stonewares. (Plates 6A,B). Perhaps, coincidentally, they appear in contexts that suggest a late seventeenth/early eighteenth century date, an attribution supported by the existence of mugs with excise pads bearing the initials WR and AR.[8] (Plate 7A). These items manifest a significant development in the formulation of glazes in that their mottled brown colouration is attributable to manganese; not present as a mere impurity, but added by the potter for a preferred effect. Plot mentions a *Motley colour*, which is procured by blending the lead and manganese by the workmen call'd *magnus*. It could not, however, be claimed that either their stylistic characteristics (the metal inspired turned bands) or the use of an artificially coloured glaze were in any sense exclusive to the Elers' influence.

What do these product types have in common, and to what extent are they significantly different from the Elers' red stonewares ? (See Appendix 2). A shared factor linking the wares described by Plot is their utilization of local clays which, as he informs us *they dig round about the Towne, all within half a mile distance.'* The glaze on all three types (slipware, iron-glazed and mottled wares) was based upon galena or the same mineral 'calcined into powder', stained with iron or manganese, and, in the case of slipware applied over decoration imparted by slip trailing. The final production stage involved placing the wares, flatwares being the exception, in 'coarse Metall'd pots' followed by firing to temperatures in the range of one thousand to eleven hundred degrees centigrade.

In the Elers case they moved into Staffordshire to have access to a clay that was necessary for a specific effect; in comparison with practices current in Burslem a production procedure that was more prescriptive than opportunistic. In other words the slip and ironglaze potters worked with what was available within their immediate area, and to an extent that access to a different range of clays might have led to equally different effects over which they would have had limited control.

The wares described by Plot were distributed by *'poor Cratemen'*.[9] It is implicit in this association, and particularly the information that they carried the goods *'on their backs,'* that before circa 1700 the potworks of Burslem were catering for local needs; realistically, given the mode of transport, within a fifty-mile radius from the town centre.[10] There is often a correlation between distribution and product sophistication. For example, for a later period there exists documentary evidence indicating that John Wedgwood, a white saltglaze potter, was shipping wares to the eastern states of North America.[11] There is also evidence of trading patterns that saw superior products being brought into the region from distant sources; in effect a reversal of John Wedgwood's overseas trade. Excavated seventeenth century material from Eccleshall Castle and Madeley Manor includes European tin-glazed earthenwares and Chinese porcelain.[12]

Although some of the Sadler site wares are decorated with patterns incorporating a tulip motif, to claim that this is directly attributable to the Elers and their Dutch background would be misleading, given that tulips were often depicted in needlework, silver, pewter and marquetry-decorated furniture from an earlier date. There are, moreover, close parallels between Staffordshire slipwares and Lambeth delftwares with similar patterns.[13]

As the items referred to by Plot were essentially technically identical with what was being made in the area less than ten years later we need to look outside the lead-glazed earthenware tradition for evidence of the Elers' influence. It is, perhaps, necessary to take into consideration the work of those Staffordshire potters named in Dwight's 1693 lawsuit, namely Aaron, Thomas and Richard Wedgwood. In a second writ, dated the 4 December, 1697 Dwight names Moses Middleton, Joshua Astbury of Shelton and Cornelius Hammersley of *Howle Ley in the Said County of Stafford.* Is it possible that it was the above named potters, rather than the Dutchmen, who alerted their fellow craftsmen in the area to the potential promised by an involvement with saltglaze manufacture ? Accordingly one might attribute to them the impetus for change that led to improvements in product quality, which in turn opened up new and wider markets. One writer on this subject has proposed that *before the Elers brothers migrated to Staffordshire, salt-glazed stoneware was already being made in the area*.[14] The Wedgwoods must have been producing a quantity of brown stoneware before 1693 for Dwight to have taken out a lawsuit. He chose not to take out a lawsuit against Francis Place of York who presumably was not making enough to threaten Dwight's monopoly. (Plate 12B).

Excavated brown salt-glazed stonewares from Burslem, Nottingham and London, which have been attributed to the first decade of the eighteenth century, share certain features with the Elers' redwares, notably raised hoops or bands at the foot and rim, decorative effects created by returning the pots when leather hard to the throwing wheel.[15] Sprigged ornamentations are the absent feature that might otherwise have reinforced an Elers connection. The post-Elers sprig ornamented wares, which appeared during the early 1740s, are traditionally associated with the names Astbury and Whieldon. (Plates 15B,C). The Astbury link was almost inevitable given Shaw's story concerning his Elers' experience. Irrespective of any possible involvement with the Bradwell Wood and its products, his lead-glazed earthenwares are, in comparison, arguably inferior. For example, a glaze was necessary to enhance the otherwise porous bodies used for the essential form, and associated reliefs. Furthermore, the latter are often crudely applied and in some cases individually incomplete.

Although not unknown slip casting was rare amongst wares made from red clay (the Elers' example being the most important exception) whether earthenware or stoneware. Cast red earthenwares, dating from the early 1740s, have, however, been found on the site of Samuel Bell's Pomona Potworks at Newcastle-under-Lyme.[16] (Plate 15A). This potter appears to have cast shapes that were impossible to form by throwing e.g. faceted teapots and square-shaped dishes. Casting, without deflocculents, is a good example of a technique that whilst being handicapped by certain limitations, such as a protracted forming stage, was, nevertheless, an acceptable substitute for practices demanding skill. When used in conjunction with white stoneware bodies, fired to high temperatures, the resulting products often reproduced the characteristics of porcelain. Certain thin cast examples are even slightly translucent when examined against a bright light. Extant red pots and excavated wasters from various sites in Stoke-on-Trent confirm a preference for thrown and hand-pressed forms. It appears that the Elers developed an unusual, and possibly for then unique, practice in order that they would be independent of outside help. If placed in the context of their Dutch origins, and supposedly foreign characteristics, we have a plausible explanation for Shaw's stories regarding their employment of *'simpletons'*, recourse to a *'mode of communication'*, and secret processes; practices that their Staffordshire neighbours would have probably interpreted in an unfavourable light.

To what then should we attribute their undeniably important role in the history of English ceramics? It might be argued that while there would appear to have been no precise imitations of their products, by any contemporary potter, they, nevertheless, inadvertently provided others with the impetus for technical progress and innovation. Their essentially practical qualifications included a knowledge of mould making, and skills in lathe turning. Whether they introduced this second innovation to others in the region is debatable because the earliest documentary evidence for the existence of a lathe appears in an inventory of stock belonging to Aaron Shaw (1714) when it was valued at 10 shillings.[17] Object analysis is not particularly helpful in determining the existence of lathe turning because most shapes pared on a potter's wheel, especially if performed in conjunction with a *'chum'*, are virtually indistinguishable from identical items that have been lathe turned.

George Elers claims that his great grandfather, John Philip associated with men of science, was a great chemist, and the intimate friend and associate of Joachim Becker, the most distinguished person in chemical researches of his time.[18] Yet with reference to what are essentially ceramic achievements one would not be justified in claiming for him any particular qualifications in the field of theoretical chemistry. For example, the brothers' working composition was a simple combination of clay with water, quite independent of any need for deflocculents. On the other hand we have evidence of efficient and impressive firing practices, for the density, hardness and surface qualities that characterize their stonewares were not simply a result of a variable and unspecific oven procedure. Iron bearing clays of the Bradwell type are prone to over vitrification and discolouration in the presence of reducing conditions, therefore accurate temperature and atmospheric control were important prerequisites for success.

In any evaluation of the Elers' achievements it is probably more revealing to set them against a wider European context. The nature of Chinese porcelain was, until the 1720s, a mystery that had defied the comprehension of experimenters since Bernardo-Buontalentis' investigations on behalf of Francesco de Medici.[19] While the painted designs on Chinese wares were appreciated for their exotic connotations and, from a European perspective meaningless symbolism, there is evidence indicating a late seventeenth/early eighteenth aesthetic for material qualities.[20] Böttger and Tschirnhausen performed a precarious series of experiments in connection with the creation of artificial gemstones, that in turn laid the foundations for the Meissen factory's later (from circa 1710) manufacture of Böttger's red stoneware. We are provided with an insight into the period's preoccupation with a gemstone-like hardness in a contemporary reference (1709) to *'eisenporcellane'*;

'..... a vessel which surpasses the hardness of porphry and is something entirely new in the world, as much on account of its brilliant polish and also for its everlasting durability ..... a very fine red vessel, which in every way equals the so-called red porcelain of the East Indies and a sort of stone which can be made to any connoisseur's choice of colours, surpassing marble and porphry in hardness and durability'.[21]

The Elers were, no doubt, alerted to the commercial potential promised by any success in imitating a Chinese product that, at the time of their earliest experiments, had few European equivalents. Some relatively inferior imitations were currently being produced in Holland by Lambertus Cleffius and Jacobus de Caluwe. Red stonewares of a better quality are attributed to their Delft contemporaries, Arij de Milde (died 1708) and Lambertus van Eenhoorn (died 1720). (Plates 9B,C).

Judged with reference to all known evidence the Elers were probably not directly responsible for any major changes in the workings of the embryonic ceramic industry of Staffordshire. Were it possible to claim for them a clear primary role in the introduction of saltglazing the verdict might prove rather different. This view does not, however, undermine their involuntary transitional status because, from an historical perspective, their work took place at the point at which it is

9A. A small turned red stoneware, teapot with applied prunus sprigging.

Height 3¹/₂ ins. (9 cms), Yixing, c.1690, China.
Courtesy Michael Gillingham.

This shows how close the Elers were at imitating the foreign imports even down to the applied decoration. [Pages 16, 17, 32].

It was Catherine of Braganza, the wife of Charles II who started the fashion for drinking tea at the British Court. She had been brought up drinking tea, as the Portuguese had been trading with China since the 16th century. However tea was only imported into Britain by the East India Company in 1678 and the earliest known British advertisement appeared in September that year in the 'Gazette' *"That Excellent and by all physitions approved China drink called by the Chineans Teha and by other Tay, alias Tee is sold at the Saltaness Head"* - a coffee house by the Royal Exchange.

9B. A turned red stoneware teapot with applied decoration made by Arij de Milde. An oval mark impressed on to the base shows a running fox surrounded by his name.

Height 4¹/₂ ins (11.5 cms), late 17th century, Holland. Courtesy Errol Manners. [Page 32].

9C. A turned red stoneware teapot with an applied prunus decoration and with a seated figure of a Budai below the spout. An embossed unicorn mark on the base is that of Lambertus van Eenhoorn.

Probably late 17th century, Holland. Courtesy Sothebys. [page 32].

The Dutch East India Company introduced Yixing red stoneware to Amsterdam in the 1670's and the pots arrived packed inside the tea for safety. The first imitations of Chinese imports were made in Holland and it was generally thought that the tea's aroma was best preserved in these red stoneware pots.These two teapots are representative of the type of redware being produced in Holland at the end of the 17th century. Whilst equalling the Chinese in quality they never achieved the fineness of the Elers' slipcast wares.

It seems that Arij de Milde went on to assist in the development of the fine red stoneware produced in Dresden from 1708 by Böttger.

10. A fine example of a red stoneware slipcast cup or capuchine decorated with applied sprigging.

Height 3 ins (7.5 cms), c.1695, Elers, probably Staffordshire. Courtesy Garry Atkins.

A similar example in the Victoria & Albert Museum is illustrated (ibid., Honey, plate IIc).

Coffee probably reached England during the early 17th century. By 1675 there was said to have been over 200 coffee houses, in London alone (the most famous being Edward Lloyd's). These little cups were therefore in great demand.

James Morley of Nottingham also made capuchines as described in his advertisement of c.1700. (Bodlian Library). An example is illustrated in English Brown Stoneware (Oswald Hildyard Hughes) page 111, which shows the lower section having a double wall.

The Oxford English Dictionary defines the English word 'Capuchin' as adopted from 16th century French, an adaptation of Italian capuccino - capuche 'a hood' (a friar of the Order of St. Francis of the new rule of 1568 so called from the sharp-pointed capuche). Could this have been Morley's interpretation of the word when referring to his little cup, describing the outer carved wall as a 'hood'?

A large inventory dated 1699 lists the effects of *'John Robins'* which includes the contents of two pot houses in Southwark producing tinglaze and stoneware. Under the title *'perfect stone ware'*

'20 doz and a half of capucheens att 2-10-0

4 doz fine capucheens at   16-0'.

'Coffees' and 'Chocoletts' are shown separately suggesting capuchine is a term to describe a shape rather than how it was used. They are also included under *'stone clay ware'* but interestingly are not mentioned in the delftware section (Post Medieval Archaeology, Vol.24, 1990, The Pickleherring Potteries, Frank Britton).

Margaret Macfarlane has suggested the word Capuchine could mean 'China cup' (the carved work deriving from the double walled 'Ling Lung' or 'Devil's work'). Another idea is that as in 'bellarmine', a nickname given to the bearded stoneware bottles, the 'capuchine' describes the same named monks who wore a brown habit pulled in at the middle with a cord in the same way as the cups are waisted.

11A. Capuchine wasters recovered from the site of Dwights' Fulham Pottery.

Height approx. 4 ins (10 cms), c.1685, John Dwight, Fulham.

Courtesy Museum of London.

11B. Two thrown saltglazed capuchines found in Clerkenwell, London in 1936.

Height 3 ins (7.5 cms), c.1700, Staffordshire. Courtesy Jonathan Horne.

Despite transport difficulties, the Staffordshire potters still managed to find a market for their wares in London against competition from the local manufacturers.

Through Dwight's various lawsuits it is known that brown stoneware was being made in Staffordshire as early as the last ten years of the 17th century.

11C. A crudely decorated tin-glazed capuchine produced either by the Vauxhall or Norfolk House potteries.

Height 3 ins (7.5 cms), 1700-1710, London, Courtesy Private Collection.

Tinglazed examples of this shape are rare. Frank Britton illustrates in London Delftware page 143 another which is probably of a similar date (earlier than published).

A marbled saltglaze stoneware capuchine made by Francis Place of York is now in the Victoria & Albert Museum. (Formerly Horace Walpole Collection).

12A. A small slipcast red stoneware mug with ring turned neck and grooved handle decorated with an applied prunus branch with flowers. Height 3$^7/_{16}$ ins (8.8 cms), c.1695, Elers, probably Staffordshire.

Courtesy Historic Deerfield Inc., (Photography by Amanda Marcello).

This shape of mug was very popular during the end of the 17th century and the first few years of the 18th century. This would have been called a *'fine gorge'*, a term which only seems to be applied to stoneware.

Several similar vessels with varying degrees of turning on the neck are illustrated (ibid., Honey, plates Ia, Ib, Iia, Ve, VIa). [Page 20, 23].

The unusually dark colour of this piece is attributable to the accidental creation of reducing conditions which have converted the body's iron content from ferric to ferruos oxide. In view of the extremely precarious nature of such a firing procedure, this should not be seen as an intentional, repeatable effect. It is not a true basaltes.

12B. A fine and rare saltglazed stoneware mug. Height 3$^1/_2$ ins (9 cms), c.1680, Francis Place, York. Courtesy Jonathan Horne.

Francis Place, who is better known as a graphic artist, was also an amateur potter, an activity noted by Walpole who at one time had an example of his work (a capuchine now in the Victoria and Albert Museum). Place started his pottery in c.1678 and was still producing in c.1694, in which year he writes *'the disapontment of ... my Pot Trade makes me more than half weary of p'jects'* He was a contemporary of John Dwight of Fulham and although he tried to emulate Dwight's achievements, there is no mention of Francis Place in Dwight's lawsuits. Perhaps Dwight didn't regard him as a commercial challenge. The marbled effect on a Dwight mug is achieved by using coloured clays, whereas this Place mug has the effect painted on. Even so, Place produced fine and delicate pots and was undeniably a very accomplished potter. This mug is one of only four documented pieces that can be claimed are by Francis Place of York (E.C.C. Trans., Vol.8, Part 2, pp.203-212). [Pages 20, 31].

13A (top left). 'A carved jug' as described in James Morley's advertisement of c.1700. This finely made piece has a double wall, the base is hollow and there is an inner lining.
Height 4 ins. (10 cms), c.1700, Morley, Nottingham. Courtesy private collection. [Pages 7, 12].
James Morley was one of the potters sued by John Dwight in 1693 for infringing his patent.

13B (top centre). A second carved jug of lighter colour and a more slender shape, also with an inner lining but with the base solid.
Height 3¾ ins. (9.5 cms), c.1700, possibly London? Courtesy Jonathan Horne. [Pages 7, 12].
Because of Morley's advertisement all carved jugs have been attributed to Nottingham but Nos. 13A and B, are quite different from each other and would appear to be from different factories. 13B is much closer
in colour and shape to 13c. Their handles are very similar and both have an extra piece of clay added under the handle. Another carved jug in the Glaisher Collection, which has very distinctive 'carving' has been attributed to Dwight. (Fitzwilliam Museum, No. G1 1191).

13C (top right). A thin stoneware *'gorge'* impressed with a WR excise mark at the base of the handle.
Height 3¾ ins (9.5cms), c.1700, Dwight, Fulham.
Courtesy Jonathan Horne. [Page 20].
The WR excise mark can be identified as a Fulham type 'E' having been found during excavations of the pottery site. The mug cannot date before 1700, but the shape was being produced in Dwight's 'fine white ware' some twenty years earlier. (Two white gorges in the Victoria and Albert Museum have silver mounts dated '1682').

13D (bottom right) A very fine thrown and turned salt-glazed stoneware jug of large size.
Height 5 ins (12.7cms), c.1695, unknown maker, English. Courtesy Chipstone Foundation. [Page 20].
It is believed that this jug was found in Staffordshire within ten miles of Bradwell Wood. However any Elers connection seems unlikely because as far as is known the Elers only slipcast their wares and would not have been capable of producing such a fine piece unless they hired a thrower. An intriguing piece which does not closely relate to the work of any known potter.

14A. 'Red' stoneware wasters excavated on the site of Dwight's Fulham Pottery, c.1675. Courtesy Museum of London. [Pages 20, 36].

These fragments represent the earliest tea wares made in England. Their texture and colour are due to the effects of reduction. Reducing conditions were a regular feature of most firings prior to improvements to kiln design from the mid eighteenth century. Unwanted reduction was very likely to occur in Dwight's box form, single firemouth kiln. This one factor may have placed restrictions on his ability to make satisfactory wares with the Bradwell clay. Given the Elers brothers obvious success in resolving such problems suggests their use of a multi firemouth (four to five) circular kiln. Accidental reduction was more easily avoided in a structure of this typically Staffordshire type.

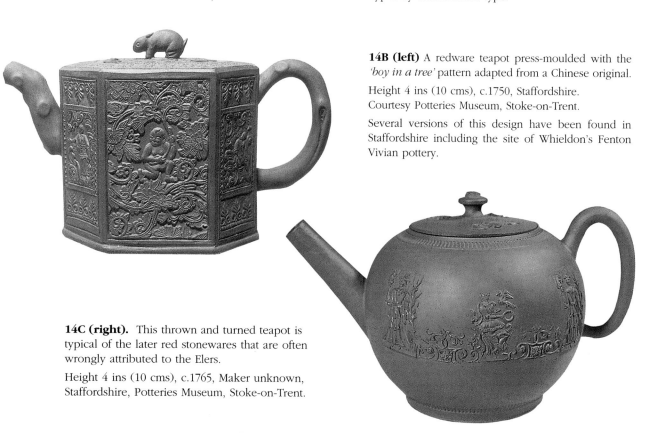

14B (left) A redware teapot press-moulded with the *'boy in a tree'* pattern adapted from a Chinese original.

Height 4 ins (10 cms), c.1750, Staffordshire.
Courtesy Potteries Museum, Stoke-on-Trent.

Several versions of this design have been found in Staffordshire including the site of Whieldon's Fenton Vivian pottery.

14C (right). This thrown and turned teapot is typical of the later red stonewares that are often wrongly attributed to the Elers.

Height 4 ins (10 cms), c.1765, Maker unknown, Staffordshire, Potteries Museum, Stoke-on-Trent.

15A (left). Lead-glazed slipcast red earthenware teapots recovered from the Pomona site.

Height 6¹/₈ ins (15.6 cms), 1724-44, Samuel Bell, Staffordshire.
(Photo David Barker). Courtesy Newcastle-under-Lyme Museum.

This is an early attempt at slipcasting by a Staffordshire potter. In comparison with the Elers ware the quality is poor but there are similarities with teapot, plate 3C. (E.C.C. Vol.9, part 3, plate 195). [Page 31].

15B (right) A lead-glazed earthenware teapot.

Height 4¹/₂ ins (12 cms), c.1745, Staffordshire. Courtesy Potteries Museum, Stoke-on Trent.

Although made some fifty years following the Elers' departure from north Staffordshire this teapot reveals evidence of their influence, in its turned form, sprigged reliefs and red composition. [Pages 23, 24, 31].

15C (left). An earthenware covered jug, the sponged manganese decoration applied under the glaze.

Height 6 ins (15 cms), c.1755, Staffordshire. Courtesy Potteries Museum, Stoke-on Trent.

Compare the grape and vine sprigged decoration with similar reliefs on the so-called 'Twyford teapot', plate 15D. [Pages 26, 31].

15D (right). The so-called 'Twyford teapot' is one of the earliest extant example of true basaltes made by the Wedgwood/Whieldon partnership.

Height 3 ins (7.5 cms), c.1758, Staffordshire. Courtesy Potteries Museum, Stoke-on-Trent.

The traditional association with Joshua Twyford was based upon the claim that he worked for the Elers at Bradwell. This view arose, in part, from the erroneous belief that the Elers made a true black stoneware. Compare with plates 15C and 16A. [Pages 24, 25, 26, 27].

16A (top left). Rare turned 'blackware' teapot in unglazed stoneware. Compare to the 'Twyford teapot', plate 15C.

Height 4¹/₂ ins. (9 cms), c.1755/60, probably Josiah Wedgwood, Staffordshire during his partnership with Whieldon. Courtesy Jonathan Horne.

The more brown than black appearance of this pot suggests an early experiment for a basaltes composition. It is almost certainly based on the use of ferric or red iron oxide, which in this state is not an effective stain for producing black, unless fired in a reducing atmosphere. [Page 25, 26].

16B (right). An experimental basaltes portrait medallion, excavated at Whieldon's Fenton Vivian site.

Height 2 ins (5 cms), c.1758, Whieldon/Wedgwood, Staffordshire. Courtesy Potteries Museum, Stoke-on-Trent. [Page 25].

16C (above right). A lead-glazed teapot often misleadingly termed 'Jackfield ware'. This example is not a Shropshire piece but was made in Staffordshire circa 1755/65. Height 4 ins (10 cms). Courtesy Potteries Musem, Stoke-on-Trent.

There was possibly confusion on Simeon Shaw's part in identifying wares of this type with basaltes and 'Egyptian black'. The same writer also misleadingly makes reference to a teapot with a black glaze and 'mole feet' in the context of a seventeenth century butter pot. [Pages 23, 24].

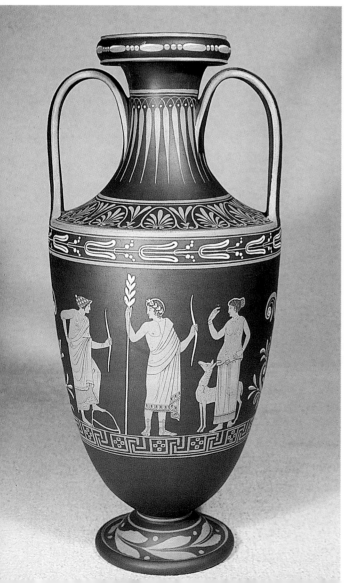

16D (bottom left). A 'Black Basalt' encaustic painted vase.

Height 16 ins (41 cms), c.1770, Josiah Wedgwood. Courtesy Potteries Museum Stoke-on-Trent.

This piece is decorated with red and white coloured enamels Contemporary archaeological discoveries and the Grand Tour made these Classical designs very popular. [Page 26].

Confusion has been caused by Enoch Wood's statement that Josiah Wedgwood was forced to abandon his patent protection for basaltes because of the competing claims of Humphrey Palmer. Wood held the mistaken belief that Wedgwood's patent (his only patent application) was for the black stoneware composition when in fact it was taken out for his encaustic decorating technique.

possible to identify advances in product quality that mark the transition from the lead-glazed earthenware stage to the appearance of technically significant stonewares.

If there is any substance in Shaw's account of the Elers it is his emphasis on the precautions taken by them to avoid the unwanted attentions of their Staffordshire neighbours. Given that he concurrently, and often, resorted to dramatic explanations for historical events, presumably in an attempt to hold the attention of his readers, also contributed to their formerly ill defined achievements.

NOTES TO CHAPTER 4

1. Dr. Robert Plot. *The Natural History of Staffordshire*. Oxford. 1686, pp.122-124. Hereafter referred to as Plot, History of Staffordshire.

2. See *Transactions of the North Staffordshire Field Club*, Vol.XCI, 1956-57 for a preliminary report on the finds from the Sadler Site, Burslem.

3. Bernard Rackham, *Medieval English Pottery*, London, Faber, 1948, p.26.

4. In North Staffordshire alone it is known that stone, and other building materials, were salvaged from abbeys and used in the construction of domestic dwellings in the immediate locality.

5. A saturated solution occurs in a glaze when, for example, a colourant, in this case iron oxide, is added in amounts that are in excess of what the glaze can completely take into solution. The streaked effect seen on some English iron-glazed wares, and the so-called hare's fur temmoku wares of Eastern China, are representative examples.

6. Opportunism in manufacture is when the potter utilizes naturally stained clays etc., in a manner that exploits their potential; usually without significant modification.

7. Plot, *History of Staffordshire*, p.122.

8. See J.H. Kelly, "A rescue excavation on the site of Swan Bank Methodist Church, Burslem", *Stoke-on-Trent Museum Archaeological Society Report*, No.5, 1973.

9. Plot, *History of Staffordshire*, p.124.

10. Brown stoneware of c.1710 has been excavated in London (Woolwich). *A catalogue of English Brown Stoneware from the 17th and 18th centuries*, Jonathan Horne, 1985, page 33.

11. For further details concerning the career of John Wedgwood see Mountford, *Staffordshire Saltglaze.*

12. These sites have revealed an interesting cross section of ceramic types that are totally in keeping with the living standards of an affluent late medieval landowner from a household consisting of servants and the served. In both cases there were connections with London, which in turn provided access to goods from a variety of sources, from the Low Countries to China.

13. For representative examples of slip and delftwares decorated with tulip motifs see Rackham, *Staffordshire Pottery*,

plates 7, 8, 10, 12, 14, 17, and Rackham, *Glaisher Collection*, plates 7c, 20b, 24a,c&f, 25b, 29b, 31b, 92a, 95c&d, 100b, 105a,b&c, colour plate X11.

14. Mountford, *Staffordshire Saltglaze*, p.10.

15. *Ibid*, pls.5, 6, 8, 9, 10, 11,12.

16. See Paul Bemrose, "The Pomona Potworks, Newcastle, Staffs: Samuel Bell, his Red Earthenware Productions 1724-44", *English Ceramic Circle Transactions,* Vol.9, part 3, London, 1975.

17. Lorna Weatherill, *The Pottery Trade and North Staffordshire 1660-1760*, Manchester University Press, 1971, Manchester, p.34.

18. *Memoirs of George Elers,* 1903.

19. The Medici workshop existed for a short period from 1575-1587. For further information on this subject see G. Liverani, *Catalogo delle porcellane dei Medici,* Faenza, 1936 and Arthur Lane, *Italian Porcelain* , London 1954. The technical aspects of Medici porcelain are discussed by W.D. Kingery and P.B. Vandiver, Ceramic Masterpieces: Art, Structure and Technology, New York, Macmillan, 1986.

20. See Comte De Milly, *L'art De La Porcelaine,* Paris, 1771.

21. Cited by W.B. Honey, *The Art of the Potter,* London, Faber, 1946, p.77, without quoting a source.

A red stoneware teabowl with applied prunus sprigging.
Height 2 ins (5 cms), c.1695
Elers, probably Staffordshire.
Courtesy Potteries Museum Stoke-on-Trent. [Page 20].

The interior of the same Elers red stoneware teabowl (left) and a red stoneware cup with handle.
Height of cups 2³/₄ins (7cms). Made in Staffordshire, c.1770.
The 17th Century teabowl shows features attributable to production by casting using a simple water slip. Compare the pin holes and sinking on the base with the more even surface exhibited by the thrown cup on the right.
Courtesy Potteries Museum, Stoke-on-Trent. [Page 20].

CHAPTER 5 : THE LAWSUITS OF
JOHN DWIGHT AND OTHER DOCUMENTARY EVIDENCE

In view of Dwight's earlier post as secretary to the Bishop of Chester, and later interest in ceramics, one may reasonably assume he would have used the opportunity to visit North Staffordshire. It is, therefore, perhaps rather surprising that the earliest reference to red clay from the area does not appear in his notebook until November 1693.[1]

Mrs. Arundell Esdaile in a paper to the English Ceramic Circle established significant links between Dwight's ecclesiastical connections and the granting of his first patent in April 1672.[2] As Bishop Wilkins of Chester was also Secretary to the Royal Society it was possibly through him that the Fulham potter's experiments were made known to King Charles II, the Society's President, and to the Vice President, Prince Rupert. Given the backing of such a distinguished trio it was almost inevitable that Dwight's patent application would prove successful. An indication of his status and growing reputation is evident in a reference by Dr. Robert Plot who writes of *the ingenious Mr. Dwight MA formerly of Christ College, Oxford,* [3] and John Houghton who mentions *the ingenious Mr.Dwight of Fulham who is interested in the properties of clays*.[4]

The Elers were cited in Dwight's 1693 lawsuit on grounds that they had employed John Chandler for the purposes of gaining an insight into production as practised at Fulham. The litigation stated that the defendants *did insinuate themselves into the acquaintance of the said John Chandler*,[5] a former employee at the Fulham pottery.It has been argued that there was something possibly unique about the Dutchmen's production procedure that when presented in evidence would have defused the validity of the lawsuit. In any event a truce between Dwight and the Elers was established possibly arising, in part, from an arrangement based on them working under licence to the patentee and that furthermore involved supplying him with the Staffordshire red clay; a theory that is reinforced by the previously mentioned recipe recorded in November 1693. There is also documentary evidence in the *Order Book* at the Public Record Office to suggest an amicable resolution to the dispute;

'Its was alleged that the other defts have since ye sd ordr for Tryall agreed with the plte soe yt ye sd Deft Morley is left solely to himself to make his defence at ye Tryall therefore and for that the sd deft Morley is noe wayes concerned in makeing or vending ye Red Tea potts'.[6]

There is additional evidence in a letter received by Sir John Lowther dated 21 March, 1697 in which it is recorded; *'He says further yt yr are a Company of Dutchmen who (by Licence from Mr. D.) make ye fine ware in Staffordshire'*[7].

If the Elers' defence of the Bill of Complaint is to be believed it is difficult to appreciate their reasons for employing Chandler given the probability that any links between the parties would become known to Dwight. In view of the importance of the Elers/Chandler connection it is necessary to consider the available documentary evidence, in particular the defendants' answer sworn on the 24 July, 1693;

'And this Deft John Chandler doth confess that he was formerly hired by the Complt to be his Servant and for some yeares imployed by him as a Labourer about the makeing and fitting of severall materialls for Earthern wares but doth deny that by means thereof he was acquainted with or acquired Skill in any measure to enable himself and the other Defts or any other person to resemble or imitate ye manufactures in the Bill menconed and further Saith that he departed from the Service of ye Complt and about Two years after Such Departure and not sooner was retained and hired to serve the said Defts David Elers and John Elers as a Labourer to fitt & prpare materialls for severall Earten wares made by them and is not otherwise concerned in the Said manufactures and doth denie that he was inticed by ye said other Deft James Morley or any or either of them to the knowledg or beleife of these Defts David Elers & John Elers did intice the Deft John Chandler to defect the Complts service or to enter into a confederacy or copartnership with them the said Defts or any of them but these Defts did agree to

make or cause to be made an authority from the Complt openly and not in a private or secrett manner made and sould severall quantities and sorts of Earthen wares commonly called Cologne or Stone ware and also wares called Red Teapotts different in nature and substance from those made by ye Complt though of a better figure and outward appearance'.[8]

Use of the designation 'labourer' is ambiguous to the extent that in a twentieth century context it suggests duties of a menial nature. However, in this instance the heavy physical aspect of clay mixing was probably carried out with reference to documented recipes, the interpretation of which demanded at least an ability to read directions and to weigh ingredients.

As there is no evidence to suggest the Elers produced saltglaze wares in Staffordshire their agreement with Dwight was possibly worked out on a basis that saw them abandon saltglaze production in London at the same time dispensing with the services of Chandler, and to supply Dwight with Staffordshire red clay. These circumstances would have signalled the premature end of their attempts to establish saltglaze production in Staffordshire.[9]

Given the long history of saltglazing in Germany and the Low Countries Dwight clearly did not invent the technique. In order to secure Letters Patent it was merely necessary to prove that no one else was already making the ware in Britain. For the Elers' part they were possibly unfamiliar with the workings of the British patent system; a situation which would explain their open infringement of Dwight's apparent monopoly. It is, therefore, not inconceivable that a plea of ignorance was offered as mitigating evidence. That saltglaze wares were produced by them at some stage is highly probable in that in replying to the lawsuit they claimed to have had experience of its production as a result of David Elers spending some *'considerable time resided for that purpose at Cologne in Germany'.*[10] (Plate I).

On the question of whether Dwight was involved in the manufacture of red stoneware there is very little evidence to suggest his commercial activity in this area, except for the existence of a few wasters recovered from the Fulham site. Taking all known evidence into consideration it is probable that while he made some experimental red wares they, nevertheless,

failed to satisfy the desired standard.[11] (Plate 14A). The few wasters from the pottery are coarse in comparison with similar fragments from Bradwell Wood and are from wares formed by throwing. Dwight's claims concerning the invention of 'opacous red' were not made until the submission of his second patent in June 1684, and while Dr. Robert Plot's account in *The Natural History of Oxfordshire,* 1677, gives a full and detailed description of the Fulham Pottery's products he makes no mention of anything that could be interpreted as a reference to red stoneware. Furthermore, the Elers in their reply to litigation dated July 28, 1693 state;

'..... & this Deft David Elers further saith that he doth not know or belive that the Complt by himself or others ever put in use or practice or ever made any of the manufactures of Earthen wares in the said Letters Patents & Bill or any of them menconed except what is and are Cologne or Stone wares and further saith & confeseth that he and the said John Elers have for about the space of three years now last past & noe longer without any lycence or authority from the Complt openly (and not in a private or secrett manner) made or caused to be made & sold severall quantityes of Brown Muggs but never did make or sell any other of the manufactures or Earthenwares in the Bill menconed or any other Earthenwares whatsoever nor imitate counterfeite or resemble the same And further saith that the said Earthen wares called red Thea potts made & sold by this Deft & the said John Elers as aforesaid were & are different in substance & shape from any of the wares or manufactures in the Complts Bill.'

This answer was followed by a further bill on the 10 August, 1693 supported by actual material evidence;

'..... the pls Councell Insisted that the defts have made severall Earthenwares contrary to the sayd 2nd Lres Patents which are now produced in Court and particularly one Browne Mugg and 2 red teapotts in Imitation of China'.[12]

It might have helped the Elers' case if they had offered in their defence evidence that their teapots were cast. If, however, Chandler or someone else was employed at this time by them as a thrower this rather significant difference in production procedure would not have existed. Irrespective of the precise circumstances Dwight and the Elers had obviously settled their dispute during the period from the 10 August and late November 1693, for a further injunction dated the 21 November was issued on which their name does not appear. Could it be that the decision to slipcast was part of the agreement to terminate John Chandler's services ? If, in addition, they had also abandoned plans to make salt-glazed stonewares, whilst paying Dwight a royalty for the use of the Bradwell clay, we have a reasonable explanation for their later unhindered activities in Staffordshire.

The next legal document in this series might suggest a strange but not entirely improbable change of relationship between plaintiff and defendant, arising out of the Elers role as a channel of information concerning their neighbours in Staffordshire; on the 15 December, 1693 a further lawsuit was filed naming three members of the Wedgwood family;

'It was alleadged that since the exhibiteing the plts bill the plt hath discovered and is advised that Aaron Wedgwood Thomas Wedgwood and Richard Wedgwood are fitt persons to be made parties to this suite It was therefore ordered yt the plt may be at Liberty to insert the said Aaron, Thomas Wedgwood & Richard Wedgwood as defts in the said Bill with apt words to charge them which this Court hold reasonable and doth order the same accordingly.' Use of the word 'advised' is perhaps revealing in this context in that it suggests the provision of information rather than a direct observation on Dwight's part.

There is an intriguing reference in the Bill of Complaint dated December 4, 1697, to a Joshua Astbury along with Moses Middleton and Cornelius Hammersley;

'..... intrudeing themselves unknown into yr Orators workhouses to inspect his furnaces and wayes of Manufacturing haveing learnt how to Counterfeit the Said manufactures thereupon they the said Confederates or Some of them by the combinacon and to the intent aforesaid and without any lycense or authority from yr Oratr have or hath for severall yeares last past in a private and secrett manner made and Sould very great quantities of Earthen Wares in imitation'.[13]
Could the Joshua Astbury named in this document have had any connection with or, in fact, been one and the same as the Astbury cited by Shaw who claims that by assuming the *'garb and appearance of an idiot'* he entered employment with the Elers' and *'had opportunity of witnessing*

every process, and examining every utensil they employed' ? Shaw makes no mention of Dwight, either because he was not directly involved in ceramic production in Staffordshire or because he was unaware of the Fulham potter's wider role in late seventeenth century English ceramics.

The bill alleges that the defendants had entered Dwight's premises presumably illegally, *'yr Orators workhouses to inspect his furnaces and wayes of Manufacturing.'* Although somewhat tenuous it is, I believe, possible that a corruption of this evidence was passed down in North Staffordshire linking Astbury and the Elers when, in fact, the intrusion was against Dwight. The Elers' connection might have arisen as a result of them exercising their new role as Dwight's legally sanctioned agents in Staffordshire. If Astbury was, indeed, making *'earthenwares ..... in a private and secrett manner ..... being far inferior to them in value and service.'* this information could have been conveyed to Dwight by the Elers.

In all probability the brothers had left Staffordshire before the end of the summer of 1698. Rhoda Edwards has published important details concerning various key stages in their movements after this date. She includes a lease agreement established in September 1698 between the owner of Bradwell Hall, Mrs. Sneyd of Keele, and a new tenant, William Beech. Given the many changes that have taken place at Bradwell Hall, especially during this century, the document provides an interesting insight into its facilities at the time of the Elers' occupancy;

'All that her (Mrs.Sneyd's) Capitall Messuage or Tenement Com(m)only Called and knowne by the name of Broadwell Hall with the Orchards Gardens Edifices Buildings Barns stables Courts Foulds and Fould Yards thereunto belonging ..... now or late were in the possession of John Elers gent'.[14]

Ms Edwards goes on to suggest that in view of the terms contained in the following paragraph the Elers were possibly evicted;

' ..... shall and will take away and pull downe and destroy a Certain Potthouse or pott oven adjoyning to the stable and now erected upon the demised p(re)mises and shall not nor will not make to suffer to be made any potts or earthen wares in the said Pott oven during the terme hereby granted.'

There is a certain irony in this condition in that

it is followed by a clause which allowed Beech '*to dig Cast up and get Clay and sand and to make Brick and tyle thereof for his and their own proper use and uses on the p(re)mises onely (but not to sell any) in the usuall place and places in Broadwell Parke and to burne the same in a Kylne now erected in the said Parke.*'[15].

In more recent times the environmental problems at Bradwell have been caused by an expansion of these very activities, namely clay quarrying and brick manufacture; a situation especially apparent during the 1970s.

That the Elers were involved in farming, concurrent with their pottery making, is a less well documented aspect of their work at Bradwell Hall, and somewhat surprising given that the farmer/potter status is more usually associated with the makers of coarser products such as the wares made by rural potteries;

'*Mr. Elers rents the house - stables Barnes etc. at Broadwell ..... he pays aforehand rent and one halfe of all Lewns and taxes and Keeps all the buildings in repairs.*' And from the same writer; '*It also gives details of his ploughing and sowing and buying of stock, from which one can conclude he was also a gentleman farmer*'.[16]

As mentioned in chapter one the Elers' bankruptcy was reported in the *London Gazette* for December 1700;

'*A Commission of Bankrupt being awarded against David Elers, and John Philip Elers, late of Foxhall in Surrey, Pot-makers; Notice is given, That Moiety and Interest of the said Bankrupts in the Workhouses at Foxhall, and the Goods and Things belonging to the said Trade, will be sold on Thursday next, the 12th. Instant ..... A Particular may be seen at the said Work house at Foxhall*'.[17]

Other dates and events relating to the Elers that post date their bankruptcy are as follows;

'1714 May; A David Elers was assessed for a church rate in the parish of St. Dionis Backchurch. He was living in Fenchurch Street'.[18]

'1714; David Elers son of David & Mary Elers Mercht., bapt. 9 Sept. St. Dionis Backchurch. This son, David's sister Anne Mary, and his daughter, Elizabeth and son Lambert, were buried in the same parish by 1721'.[19]

David Elers appears in a register of sales as a purchaser of oriental wares from the East India Company. He was re-exporting these items to Dublin, presumably to his brother, John Philip.[20]

NOTES TO CHAPTER 5

1. See Haselgrove and Murray, *Dwight*, for a facsimile of Dwight's *Commonplace Book*.

2. Mrs. Arundell Esdaile, "Further Notes on John Dwight", *English Ceramic Circle Transactions*, Vol. 11, No.6, 1939, pp.40-48.

3. Dr. Robert Plot, *The Natural History of Oxfordshire*, Oxford, 1677, pp.84-88.

4. John Houghton, *Essays on Husbandry and Trade*, 1693.

5. Dwight's first lawsuit, dated 20th. June, 1693, citing John Chandler, John Philip Elers, David Elers and James Morley. For a full transcript see Haselgrove and Murray, Dwight.

6. *Public Records Office Order Book*, C33/281, F.39 and litigations taken out by Dwight citing James Morley but omitting the Elers, dated 21st. November, 1693. See Haselgrove and Murray, *Dwight*.

7. *Ibid*, p.144, letter of Sir John Lowther, 21st. March, 1697.

8. *Ibid*.

9. The lawsuits reinforce the probability that the Elers were involved with saltglaze production during their London phase. (Plate I).

10. Answer for Chandler and Elers, sworn by Chandler and David Elers, 24th. July, 1693. See Haselgrove and Murray, *Dwight*, pp.90-91.

11. It is clear from an entry in Dwight's notebook for 1695 that he was, at least, experimenting with wares made from red clay; '*The little furnace where the last red Teapots were burnt, I take to be a convenient one for this Use*'. *Ibid*, pp.74-75.

12. *Ibid*, pp.95-96.

13. *Ibid*, pp.122-124.

14. Rhoda Edwards, "London Potters circa 1570-1710", *Journal of Ceramic History*, No.6, Stafford, George Street Press, 1974.

15. *Ibid.*, p.62.

16. *Ibid*.

17. *Ibid*.

18. *Ibid*.

19. *Ibid*.

20. *Ibid* .

Bradwell Hall, photographed in 1997

APPENDIX 1 :
Bradwell Hall in 1997

After a twenty year absence I re-visited Bradwell Hall in January 1997. I have now seen the house and its surroundings in three distinctly different states. In the mid 1950s it was still operating as a working farm, situated in open fields on the Burslem side, mixed with what remained of the wood. In 1976 the landscape had changed very much for the worsed for the whole of the site was by then totally taken over by the activities of clay excavation and brick crushing; the Bradwell clay being used at this time for the manufacture of hard red floor tiles

The circumstances that led to its current third phase were, in part, created by a fall off in demand for aggregates by local industry. Bradwell Hall is today used as an old people's home. Virtually all traces of its industrial past have been removed and the clay pit that once dominated the site has been filled up and levelled. The Twigge family connection is currently being maintained by the sons of the Mr. Twigge I met there in the 1950s. They have restored the hall and some of its most interesting features. Parts of the original oak staircase are still in situ and the Sneyd family coat of arm.s (in one of the bedrooms) has been cleaned and repainted, not in its original polychrome but in emulsion paint. The staircase is difficult to date precisely but may conceivably have been part of the earliest dwelling. The coat of arms is thought to date from the mid seventeenth century. Protected by a glass panel is a section of the original wattle and daub construction, while the lower rooms contain early twentieth century panelling recovered from Longton Town Hall.

It is claimed that the Sneyd family occupied a house at Bradwell as early as 1401. John Ward (*A History of the Borough of Stoke-upon-Trent, 1843*) provides a genealogical table (pp.82-83) identifying '*William Sneyde, of Tunstall and Bradwell, A.D. 1402.*' The same writer cites Robert Plot who, in an unidentified publication of 1670, allegedly described the hall as showing '*a great deal of present or of past magnificence.*'

Ward goes on to comment that *'The mansion has been principally pulled down, and the extensive deer-park ..... disparked).* The present structure, which is stylistically of an early nineteenth century date, has been constructed to enclose parts of the original house, as evidenced by the wattle and daub walls and Sneyd family crest.

The area immediately adjoining two sides of the main building is now occupied by single story dwellings, recently built to accommodate the residents of Bradwell Hall Nursing Home. I was told that despite extensive excavations for footings no evidence of its ceramic past was revealed. Work on a nearby housing estate was similarly unproductive. Given that the footings for most of the buildings were dug to little more than two to three feet it is possible that any archaeological material may have simply remained undisturbed. In view of the newness of these properties, and the buildings immediately on three sides of the hall, the opportunites for further investigation must remain in the very distant future.

APPENDIX 2 :
Object Analysis: Elers' red stoneware and late seventeenth century lead-glazed earthenwares

The differences that separate the slipwares somewhat sketchily referred to by Plot, and products identified with the Elers, may be divided under the following headings;

1. Market level

2. Refinement of finish

3. Body quality

4. Stylistic origins

5. The presence and absence of additions to the main form whether permanently attached or removable e.g. the differences between a spout and lid.

6. Complexity of the firing process - once or twice fired.

While the Elers' red stonewares reveal negligible variations in quality the following comparative exercise is based upon the best examples of late seventeenth century lead-glazed earthen-wares.

MARKET LEVEL; Plot's reference to cratemen suggests a distribution pattern that was limited to neighbouring counties e.g. Shropshire and Cheshire.

REFINEMENT OF FINISH; It is important to differentiate between the application of surface decoration, which might also hide the underlying body thus, perhaps, concealing a clay of inferior quality, and instances where ultimate effect was due to well regulated finishing processes and a refined composition.

BODY QUALITY; Slipwares were totally dependent on the availability of clays with natural, fortuitous characteristics; an approach to production that may be defined as opportunistic. By applying a surface engobe, that had previously been subjected to sieving, it was possible to conceal a less refined material. Was the use of a glaze optional or necessary ? or essential as in the case of slipware.

STYLISTIC ORIGINS; The surface patterns used on Staffordshire slipware are either naturalistic or abstract e.g. a tulip motif or a marbled/ feathered effect. Forms were normally determined by functional requirements. In certain rare instances shapes were adapted from silver or pewter patterns.

Decorative categories; naturalistic; the human form, animals e.g. lions and birds, flowers. Inscriptions; dedications *'The best is not too good for you',* partisan e.g. *'No Pope',* individual names either of maker or recipient. Abstract; mainly marbling with slips of two or more colours, feathering or combing by drawing a bristle or wire through wet slip.

THE PRESENCE AND ABSENCE OF ADDITIONS TO THE MAIN FORM; Handles on cups, porringers and posset pots. Diminutive spouts are known on some posset pots. Lidded vessels in slipware are rare and limited to posset and honey pots.

Teapots are unknown in seventeenth century Staffordshire slipware, and small drinking vessels were for ale, sack and water. Uniform and technically refined appendages would have depended on an appropriate mould technology which, at this stage in the trade's development, did not exist.

COMPLEXITY OF THE FIRING PROCESS; A single firing that fused body and glaze, and to temperatures below eleven hundred degrees centigrade. Saggars were, according to Plot, used in conjunction with the firing of superior hollowares. The same wares were also placed on 'bobs'. Firing temperatures were not of critical importance and soaking (prolonged exposure to a constant, generally high temperature) was also non essential. There is evidence for unintentional rapid cooling in connection with iron glazes, hence a crystal glaze structure.

Elers' red stoneware

MARKET LEVEL; Their products were intended for an affluent market familiar with Chinese porcelain and red stoneware of the Yixing type.

REFINEMENT OF FINISH; Well engineered forms, light in weight, with a superior surface finish, generally ornamented with separately moulded reliefs.

BODY QUALITY; Dense, hard, smooth, free from undesirable impurities. Prepared by careful sieving.

STYLISTIC ORIGINS; Inspired by Chinese stoneware and European silver forms. Use of prunus blossom reliefs similar to those found on blanc de-chine porcelain and some unglazed stonewares. An awareness of decorative styles from sources external to Britain and the Netherlands.

ATTACHMENTS AND REMOVABLE COMPONENTS; Spouts and well-engineered lids on teapots. Close fitting metal stoppers on perfume bottles. Matching tea bowls and saucers. Complexity of the firing process: Firing to stoneware temperatures in excess of eleven hundred degrees centigrade.

Body density suggests use of a soaking period.

Accurate atmospheric control in the interests of body colour and the avoidance of unintentional reduction.

Kiln furniture - unnecessary.

Saggars - advantageous.

APPENDIX 3 :
Martin Lister and John Houghton

A communication to the Royal Society by Martin Lister F.R.S. from the Royal Society Philosophical Transaction,.17, 1693, p.699.

'This is meant of the soft Oar like Clay. I have this to add, that this Clay, Haemitites is as good, if not better, that that which is brought from the East Indies. Witness the Tea-Pots now to be sold at the Potters in the Poultry in Cheapside which not only for Art, but for beautiful colour too, are far beyond any we have from China. These are made of the English Haemitites in Staffordshire, as I take it, by two Dutch-men incomparable Artists.'

'Advertisement' in John Houghton F.R.S. *'Husbandry and Trade Improv'd'.* *'There is found near Faux-hall in Surrey, a sort of Clay used to make all sorts of Tea Pots, well approved of by most Toy-Shops about the Exchange, and are hardly discerned from China, and other Pots from beyond the Sea, being very exact in Colour, Strength, and Shape, and lately applied to this use by two Dutch Brothers whose mames are Eelers, John Houghton, 13 Oct, 1693.'*

Martin Lister (1638-1712) was born into a Yorkshire family which had produced several members distinguished for their contributions to medicine. Son of Sir Martin Lister (knighted 1625) he received his early education from an uncle, Sir Matthew Lister, before going on to St. John's College, Cambridge at the young age of sixteen. Graduating with a B.A. in 1658-9 he was made a fellow of his college in 1660 and received an M.A. in 1662. Lister was first and foremost a zoologist, yet in the diversity of his interests and knowledge he was a true Renaissance man contributing regularly to the *Philosophical Transactions* with papers, about forty in number, on meterology, minerals, molluscs, medicine, and antiquities.

Official recognition came in 1670-71 when he was elected a Fellow of the Royal Society. At a later stage he went on to study medicine followed by the establishment of a practice in York. It was during this period that Lister developed an interest in antiquites, possibly as a result of the city's Roman past. Although it is not known how they came into his possession he made several important gifts to the Ashmolean Museum, Oxford, of Roman altars and coins.

Further academic awards followed; an M.D. from the university of Oxford in 1684 and fellowship of the Royal College of Physicians in 1687. A wider reputation resulted from the publication of his *Historia Sive Synopsis Methodica Conchyliorum* 1685-92. 1685 also saw the appearance of a shorter work *Historia Conchyliorum.*

Lister died at Epsom 2 February, 1712, and was buried in Clapham Church.

John Houghton (died 1705) studied for a time at Corpus Christi College, Cambridge, followed by a period as a writer on agriculture and trade. His career took a change of direction when he became an apothecary and dealer in tea, coffee and chocolate first *'against the Ship Tavern in St. Bartholomew Lane, behind the Royal Exchange'*, and later (1703) at the *'Golden Fleece at the corner of Little Eastcheap in Gracechurch Street'*, London. Houghton's reference to the Elers was as a result of a parallel occupation as the seventeenth century equivalent of a manufacturers' agent, and editorship of a periodical entitled *A Collection of Letters for the Improvement of Husbandry and Trade*, 1681-83. This later became *'A Proposal for the Improvement of Husbandry and Trade'*,. appearing from 30 March, 1692, in the form of weekly editions. He too was elected a Fellow of the Royal Society on the 29 January, 1680, serving for a time on the Society's committee for agriculture. His other published works include 'A Discourse of Coffee', *Philosophical Transactions* Vol. XX1 311-317 and 'The Conclusion of the Protestant, States of the Empire, of the 23d. of September 1699 concerning the Calendar', *Philosophical Transactions* Vol.XX11, 459-463.

APPENDIX 4
Synopsis of Wedgwood's Patent for Encaustic Painting from Patents for Inventions. Abridgements of the Specifications Relating to Pottery

Professor Bennet Woodcroft, Superintendent of Specifications, London, 1863.

'A.D. 1769, November 16, No.939

Wedgwood, Josiah ..... The purpose of ornamenting earthen and porcelaine ware with an encaustic gold bronze, together with a peculiar species of encaustic painting in various colours in imitation of the antient Etruscan and Roman earthenware. In carrying out this invention, the patentee first prepares ten ingredients, among which is bronze powder; some of these are one chemical substance, whilst others are composed mostly of several chemical substances in certain proportions, and generally calcined together. The substances used are Ayoree, a white earth of North America, gold, aqua regia, copper, oxide of antimony, tin ashes (oxide of tin), white and red lead, smalts, borax, nitre, copperas, flint, manganese, and zaffer. By mixing these ingredients, with the exception of the bronze powder, in different proportions, he obtains seven colours, which he names as follows: Red, orange, dry black, white, green, blue, yellow, and he produces another colour, which he names shineing black, by mixing some of these ingredients and one of the colours, namely, the green.

In applying the bronze powder, grind some of it in oil of turpentine, and apply this by sponge or pencil to the vessels finished, ready for burning, but not quite dry, polish it; heat the ware as high as is necessary for it; afterwards burnish the bronze. Applying the bronze after the ware is fired bisket, make a mixture in certain proportions of white lead and calcined ground flint, grind them well together; apply this thin with a sponge or brush, flux it, then apply upon it the bronze as before directed.

Shineing black (and other colours) upon red vessels, antique Etruscan vases. These colours are ground with oil of turpentine before applying them to the vessels, and are proceeded with as in the first application of the bronze powder.'

APPENDIX 5:
Marks on seventeenth century red stonewares

Makers of red stoneware in Holland often identified their products with animal symbols impressed into the pre-fired body. Examples include the running fox of de Milde, the hind of de Calawe, and the unicorn of van Eenhorn. A small number of Elers' wares exist on which there are imitation Chinese seal marks (Figs. 1, 2 & 3). It is difficult to offer an explanation for the fact that these marks were applied to a few Elers' products whilst being absent on the majority. Given that they occur on particularly fine examples might indicate a date of manufacture at a point towards the end of their tenancy of Bradwell Hall, in other words during the years 1696-98. Although normally appearing as an impressed seal on the base of wares the British Museum has a handleless cup with all three marks used as decoration on the vessel wall. (Illustrated by W.B. Honey, 'Elers' Ware', Transactions of the English Ceramic Circle No.2, 1934, plate 111 c.).

Fig. 1.

Fig. 2.

Fig. 3.

W.B. Honey has commented on the temptation to regard the mark in fig.2 as a disguised rendering of the initials 'J.E.', a proposition that he goes on to rule out. The combination of slip casting appearing in conjunction with stylistic features attributable to the seventeenth century, and a seal mark or marks matching those illustrated in figs. 1-3 is confirmation of an Elers origin.

APPENDIX 6:
Will and Inventory of Theodore or Dirck Elers

Philippa Glanville has brought to notice this important document comprising the will and inventory for probate of Theodore or Dirck Elers, a merchant of St. Mary le Bow in the City of London, 1693. The will details legacies in china and 'lackery' ware left to his nephews Martin, David, John Philip and Theodore Elers.

The inventory of his goods lists the china wares in his possession at his death and includes *'boxes, trunkes & other sortes of several seizes and shapes, square, round, ovell and other sortes, blew and white mixt colours, blew and guilded and ingraven and dishes to the number of 1013 (valued at £222.16s) ... 12 chestes of China basons or large cuppes and 13 chestes of small China tea cuppes (valued at £556.15s).'*

This document is of importance as it shows that the brothers John Philip and David Elers had family connections with the china importing trade. Indeed, this connection may have prompted their earliest experiments.

(Catalogue of an Exhibition of recent gifts and accessions 1950-60. Published by The Church Information Office, 1960.)

BIBLIOGRAPHY

AIKEN, John A Description of the Country from Thirty to Forty Miles Round Manchester, 1795

ARUNDELL ESDAILE, MRS., "Further Notes on John Dwight", English Ceramic circle Transactions, Vol.II, No.6, 1939, pp.40-48

BEMROSE, PAUL, "The Pomona Potworks, Newcastle, Staffs: Samuel Bell, his Red Earthenware Productions 1724-44", English Ceramic Circle Transactions, Vol.9, part 3, 1975

BIMSON, MAVIS "John Dwight", English Ceramic Circle Transactions, Vol. V, Part 2, 1961, pp.95-109

BURTON, WILLIAM, A History and Description of English Earthenware and Stoneware, London, Cassell, 1904

EDWARDS, RHODA, "London Potters circa 1570-1710", Journal of Ceramic History, No.6, 1974

EDWARDS, DIANA, Black Basalt: Wedgwood and Contemporary Manufacturers, Woodbridge, Antique Collectors' Club, 1994

FINER, ANN AND SAVAGE, GEORGE, The Selected Letters of Josiah Wedgwood, London, Cory, Adams & Mackay, 1965

GRANT, M.H., The Makers of Black Basaltes, 1910

HASELGROVE, D. AND MURRAY, J., "John Dwight's Fulham Pottery 1672 1978; A Collection of Documentary Sources", Journal of Ceramic History, No.XL, 1979

HONEY, W.B., "Elers' Ware", Transactions of the English Ceramic Circle, No.11, 1934

JEWITT, L., The Ceramic Art of Great Britain, Poole, New Orchard Editions, 1985

JEWITT, L., The Wedgwoods: Being a Life of Josiah Wedgwood, London, Virtue, 1865

KELLY. J.H., "A rescue excavation on the site of Swan Bank Methodist Church, Burslem," Stoke-on-Trent Museum Archaeological Society Report, No.5, 1973

MORRIS, G.C., The Journeys of Celia Fiennes, 1947

MORTON, E.J., Letters of Josiah Wedgwood 1771-1780

MOUNTFORD, A.R., Staffordshire Salt-glazed Stoneware, London, Barrie and Jenkins, 1971

MOUNTFORD, A.R "Thomas Whieldon's Manufactory at Fenton Vivian", Transactions of the English Ceramic Circle, Vol.8, Part 2, 1972, pp.164-182

PLOT, ROBERT, The Natural History of Oxfordshire, 1677

PLOT, ROBERT, The Natural History of Staffordshire, 1686

RACKHAM, BERNARD, Catalogue of the Glaisher Collection of Pottery and Porcelain in the Fitzwilliam Museum, Cambridge, Cambridge, 1935

RACKHAM, BERNARD, Early Staffordshire Pottery, London, Faber, 1951

RACKHAM, BERNARD, AND READ, HERBERT, English Pottery, London, Ernest Benn, 1974

RHEAD, G.W. AND F.A., Staffordshire Pots and Potters, London, Hutchinson, 1906

SHAW, SIMEON, History of the Staffordshire Potteries, Hanley, 1829

SOLON, L.M., The Art of the Old English Potter, London, Bemrose, 1885

WEATHERILL, LORNA, The Pottery Trade and North Staffordshire 1660-1760, Manchester, Manchester University Press, 1971

WEDGWOOD, J.C., Staffordshire Pottery and its History, London, Sampson Low, Marston, 1913

INDEX